P9-CKD-178

Spectacle Pedagogy

700.103
G190

WITHDRAWI

Spectacle Pedagogy

Art, Politics, and Visual Culture

LIBRARY ST. MARY'S COLLEGE

Charles R. Garoian
and
Yvonne M. Gaudelius

STATE UNIVERSITY OF NEW YORK PRESS

Published by
State University of New York Press, Albany

© 2008 State University of New York

All rights reserved

Printed in the United States of America

No part of this book may be used or reproduced in any manner whatsoever
without written permission. No part of this book may be stored in a retrieval
system or transmitted in any form or by any means including electronic,
electrostatic, magnetic tape, mechanical, photocopying, recording, or
otherwise without the prior permission in writing of the publisher.

For information, contact State University of New York Press, Albany, NY
www.sunypress.edu

Production by Marilyn P. Semerad
Marketing by Susan M. Petrie

Library of Congress Cataloging-in-Publication Data

Garoian, Charles R., 1943–
   Spectacle pedagogy: art, politics, and visual culture / Charles R. Garoian,
Yvonne M. Gaudelius.
      p. cm.
   Includes bibliographical references and index.
   ISBN 978–0–7914–7385–6 (hardcover : alk. paper)
   ISBN 978–0–7914–7386–3 (pbk. : alk. paper)
   1. Art and popular culture. 2. Art and society. 3. Mass media—
Social aspects. I. Gaudelius, Yvonne II. Title.

N72.S6G375 2008
700.1′03—dc22
                                                                    2007024992

10   9   8   7   6   5   4   3   2   1

Contents

Illustrations

Acknowledgments

With these heartfelt words we would like to thank those who inspired, generously supported, and assisted us during the writing of this book. In particular, we thank Richard (Dick) Durst, President of Baldwin Wallace College and former Dean of the College of Arts and Architecture at The Pennsylvania State University who urged us to complete it in spite of our full time jobs as university administrators.

Our writing and teaching would not have been possible without the inspiration provided by the artists, theorists, and educators whose images, ideas, and teachings appear throughout the pages of this book. Their cultural work has enabled us to understand the role of art and pedagogy as important aspects of critical citizenship within contemporary culture.

The College of Arts and Architecture and the School of Visual Arts at Penn State provided funding support for us to present versions of some of these essays at national and international conferences. Additionally, the college financially supported the final stages of the manuscript through the office of Associate Dean Gunalan Nadarajan.

We acknowledge the audiences who attended our conference sessions and engaged us in dialogue by raising important questions and providing insightful comments that helped us refine our arguments.

The following individuals and agencies gave permission to publish the images included in this book: artists James Kesterke, Stacy Levy, Cristin Millett, Alexandra Sullivan, and David Young; artists Matthew Goulish and Lin Hixson of the Goat Island collective; artist and photographer Rob Martin; photographer Claude Giger; artist Krzysztof Wodiczko and archivist Stephanie Joson of Galerie Lelong in New York City; Hetty Wessels, archivist in the Reproduction Department of The Stedelijk Museum in Amsterdam, The Netherlands; artist Bill Viola and archivist David Politzer of The James Cohan Gallery in New York City; and, the Photofest, Inc., and Getty Images archives. We are also grateful to Rob Martin, who designed the concept for the cover of this book.

We also acknowledge each other as colleagues, and we recognize how important the collaborative process has been to this project. It has pushed and challenged our questions and interpretations. It was within the in-between spaces of our individual understandings that the collage of our ideas about art and culture resonated and from which the critique of spectacle culture in this book evolved.

Finally, and most important, this book would not have been possible without the steadfast support of our families. Thank you, Nigel, Sherrie, Julia, Jason, and Stephanie for your love and belief in us.

Introduction

In this collage of essays, written in the shadow of 9/11 and the ongoing war in Iraq, we examine the multiple and complex interrelationships among art, politics, and visual culture through the concept of spectacle pedagogy. We claim that contemporary artists use the strategies of collage, montage, assemblage, installation, and performance art to create volatile spaces within their artwork. As critical approaches these genres represent significant means through which art students can learn to create immanent critiques of the spectacle of visual culture through art making.

Because the postmodern condition is pervasively mediated by visual culture, our awareness of its dominating assumptions and our ability to expose, examine, and critique the spectacle of visual culture make the critical pedagogy of collage, montage, assemblage, installation, and performance art all the more imperative. When students understand the critical and paradoxical relationships between their art-making activities and the *habitus* of institutionalized schooling, between the images and ideas that they create through art and the spectacle pedagogy of visual culture, then a liminal in-between space opens that enables the potential of art-making for transgressive and transformative experiences. This collage of essays can be read in any order because just as we claim that collage, montage, assemblage, installation, and performance art are constituted by disjunctive yet coexisting fragments of cultural memory and history, so too these collage fragments represent our thoughts on culture, politics, spectacle, and pedagogy in our post–9/11 world.

The first essay, "The Embodied Pedagogy of War," was written in March 2003 as we sat huddled over the computer preparing a paper on the obsolete body of art education for presentation at the National Art Education Association (NAEA) conference in Minneapolis. When we began, the war on Iraq had not yet begun, but it was daily becoming a reality. The buzz of the

1

impending war resonated louder and louder as we lived and worked, not in a mythical ivory tower isolated from the world, but in the midst of 24–7 media coverage of the imminent attack. We soon relized, as did most of the world, that it was no longer a question of whether we would attack Iraq but rather when we would do so. As of this writing the question remains: how long will the war continue? By the time of the NAEA conference the war had begun and ignoring it in our presentation was no longer possible. As we were writing about *the* body and embodiment for our conference paper, *our* bodies were absorbing the vicarious impacts of the war in such ways that to ignore it in our presentation would have been to deny the truth. The impact of the war also led us to the performative response in this essay. As art educators and performance studies scholars we felt the necessity to pose a performative question that would enable us to open indeterminate spaces. This ambiguity, which sits in such marked contrast to the deterministic logic of waging war, enabled us to examine critically the outbreak of war. In the same way that the wetness on our cheeks is the first sign that alerts us to the fact that we are crying before we have even realized it, our bodies responded to the war, alerting us in visceral ways that we would not otherwise have recognized.

In the second essay, "The Spectacle of Visual Culture," we characterize the ideology of visual culture as "spectacle pedagogy," arguing that images are among the forms that teach us what and how to see and think and, in doing so, they mediate the ways in which we interact with one another as social beings. Given that we are always already immersed in visual culture, an understanding of its impact on social relations enables art teachers and their students to distinguish between corporate, institutionalized expressions of a clichéd or objectified "self" and expressions and creations of subjectivity through art making. Although the critique of the former promotes a narcissistic fixation with the dominant order of visual culture, the latter allows students to challenge commodity fetishism through the plurality of the personal. To enable such multiplicity in the art classroom, we propose the conceptual strategies of collage, montage, assemblage, installation, and performance art as processes through which we can expose, examine, and critique the spectacle of visual culture. Through the indeterminate modes of address of these media, students' creative and political subjectivity and agency is immanently possible as they learn to engage the spectacle politics of visual culture as critical citizens.

"The Impossible Task as Ecological Imperative," the third essay, written the week following the 9/11 attack, explores the impossible, enigmatic, and interventionist strategies of the Chicago-based performance art collective Goat Island, and their critical reading of ecological devastation as a form of terrorism as articulated through their performance *The Sea & Poison*. Given that terrorism in all of its manifestations, including those of 9/11, represents "war" perpetrated on the all encompassing "body," the body human, the body politic, and the body earth, Goat Island's "ecoperformance" *The Sea & Poison* challenges our understanding of images and their power to affect our lives and the life of the planet. In this essay we question the ethical differences between the conceptual, emotional, and physical collisions Goat Island performed and those of the 9/11 terrorists. Unlike the hypnotic assault of mass mediated entertainment, the images, ideas, and actions that are an integral part of performances such as *The Sea & Poison* enable critical reflection and social responsibility. The physical and conceptual challenges in Goat Island's work "make possible" a liminal, contingent, and ephemeral space, within which social and historical assumptions, commodity fetishism, the stereotypical representations of mass mediated culture, and the limits of knowledge can be exposed, examined, and critiqued through performance art.

Cultural theorist Gregory Ulmer (1983) claims that "collage is the single most revolutionary formal innovation in artistic representation to occur" in more than a century (p. 84). In Essay Four, "Art Education in the Silent Gap of Visual Culture," we explore the disjunctive narrative of collage and the ways in which its radical juxtaposition of images, ideas, objects, and actions is employed in the genres of cinema, photomontage, assemblage, video art, installation art, and performance art. Given the position of collage as a visual form used to entice consumption, it is, not coincidently, the most widely used mode of address by the mass mediated systems of television, advertising, the news, the movies, and the Internet. In addition, considering the surfeit of visual material available in newspapers, magazines, and other forms of visual culture, virtually every classroom teacher has employed collage as a quick, easy, and inexpensive image-making process for students to illustrate what they learn in various academic disciplines in school. A visit to a public school would give us a learning environment replete with social studies collages, arithmetic collages, language collages, health collages, and even physical education collages, in addition to using this genre in art classes. Such ubiquity notwithstanding, we find little evidence that the aesthetic dimension and disjunctive narrative of collage is understood at any depth in schools. In this essay we discuss the silent, empty gaps, the exposed, in-between dimensions of collage where a critical pedagogy is possible, where students can learn to examine and critique the academic knowledge of schooling, and where they can learn to imagine and create new cultural possibilities. Rather than merely doling out information, capturing a scene, recording history, or telling a story, the aim of collage narrative is to raise critical questions thereby generating new cultural discourse through art.

Essay Five, "The Misfit Pedagogy of Visual Culture: A Depraved Obsession with Pictures," begins with a performance narrative about the uncritical, objectifying eye of photography to characterize and examine the collaged images of abuse at Abu Ghraib prison in Iraq to critique the mass media spectacle of visual culture. The mass mediated, globalized images of al-Qaeda's terrorists attacks of 9/11, the U.S. bombing of Afghanistan, the hunt for Osama Bin Laden, and several other representations of global terrorism will be dealt with in this essay. Our purpose in examining these media displays has been to critique our collective obsession with the pastiche of spectacle culture and to suggest that a similar intervention into its narrative structure, the in-between spaces of its disparate, misfit-ting images and ideas, represents critical pedagogy in art education.

In Essay Six, "Curriculum and Pedagogy as Collage Narrative," we theorize collage to examine its narrative structure as a form of critical pedagogy in art education. Assuming its criticality, collage represents a significant means by which to conceptualize and challenge the seductive yet oppressive regimes of spectacle culture. For philosopher Thomas Brockelman (2001), the undecideablity of collage narrative, its "representational and antirepresentational" character, is "an emblem for contemporary culture" (p. 7). Considering that it is arguably the most important contribution of the twentieth century to the history of art, why has collage not received the kind of critical pedagogical attention that it deserves in the field of art education? What is the principle of collage? How is it constructed? What are its cognitive operations? What is the significance of its disjunctive form? What is the epistemology of collage and how does it function pedagogically? What impact can an art education based on collage pedagogy have on students' ability to critique the mass mediated spectacle of visual culture? Considering its eccentric epistemology, the dialectical tension of collage narrative provides insight into the interplay between curriculum and pedagogy—what we teach and how we teach it. This curriculum/pedagogy dialectic suggests "curriculum as collage," "pedagogy as collage," and their "interplay as collage." Conversely, the narrative of collage may be considered as curricular in its structure and pedagogical in its process. Given such metaphoric correspondences, the disjunctive narrative of collage suggests the "impossibility" of curriculum and pedagogy as opposing binaries.

We theorize the teleological pedagogy of visual culture in Essay Seven, "The Spectre of Visual Culture and the Hauntology of Collage," as a "haunting" that occurs, a "spectre" that inhabits the "in-between," interstitial spaces of the disparate and disjunctive images and texts of visual culture—its collage aesthetic. Although the collage spaces of visual culture are ordinarily haunted by the historically and socially constructed ideologies of commodity fetishism, government intervention, and institutionalized schooling, we argue that the undecidable, mutable characteristics of these spaces enable radical forms of intervention to occur, a haunting that challenges the ideological "specter of mass mediated culture" with the "specter of critical citizenship." Building on the hauntological theories of art historian Nicholas Mirzoeff and critical theorists Jacques Derrida and Pierre Bourdieu, such intervention and resistance represents the critical pedagogy of collage—an imperative for art education found throughout the history of modern and contemporary art yet overlooked by art education theorists and practitioners.

In our final essay, "The Dis-eased Pedagogy of Disaster Tourism," we conceptualize the virtual/virulent regime of spectacle culture as "disaster tourism" and argue against pathologizing pedagogies such as art therapy, which objectify and represent the body as the site/sight of medical science. Instead we favor the infirmed body's critical and creative expressions of subjectivity through art as an effective means of its healing and attainment of political agency within contemporary cultural life. Following cultural theorist Jean Baudrillard we purposely conflate the "virtuality" of information systems and the "virality" of the body suggesting, ironically, that both are dis-eased. The concept of "dis-ease" as we use it is double coded. On the one hand, we are referring to the disabling of the body's agency and health due to its marginalization as "objectified other" within the scopic regime of spectacle culture. On the other hand, we are referring to the enabling of the body's agency through its eccentric and reflexive examination and critique of the centric, oppressive cultural assumptions of mass mediated culture. Such critical examination constitutes a dis-eased pedagogy of resistance, a counterspectacle that challenges the virulent power of mass culture.

The Embodied Pedagogy of War

In a darkened room in the Minneapolis convention center in March 2003, the two of us stood facing each other. The floor was covered, littered, with newspapers; their 64-point headlines reporting about the "progress" of the war. A single harsh light shone diagonally through the space, illuminating us while casting a pall of long oblique shadows. In droning voices we began by repeatedly spelling out the words "planned obsolescence" in unison. We alternated the remaining parts of the narrative to represent the fragmentation of our bodies by the technology of war. Like the reporting of the news, which describes the colonization of the body by war, "imbedded" within the text of the narrative are excerpts from Wired *magazine (Harper, 2002, pp. 54–55), describing the colonization of the body by the most recent developments in medical technology.*

P - L - A - N - N - E - D - O - B - S - O - L - E - S - C - E - N - C - E - P -
L - A - N - N - E - D - O - B - S - O - L - E - S - C - E - N - C - E - P - L -
A - N - N - E - D - O - B - S - O - L - E - S - C - E - N - C - E - P - L - A -

---

This essay was originally written for a presentation for the National Art Education Association Annual Convention in Minneapolis, Minnesota, April 2003, and later published in 2004 in the National Art Education Association Social Theory Caucus *Journal of Social Theory in Art Education* 27, 62–80.

N-N-E-D-O-B-S-O-L-E-S-C-E-N-C-E-P-L-A-
N-N-E-D-O-B-S-O-L-E-S-C-E-N-C-E-P-L-A-
N-N-E-D-O-B-S-O-L-E-S-C-E-N-C-E-P-L-A-N
-N-E-D-O-B-S-O-L-E-S-C-E-N-C-E-P-L-A-N-
N-E-D-O-B-S-O-L-E-S-C-E-N-C-E-P-L-A-N-
N-E-D-O-B-S-O-L-E-S-C-E-N-C-E-P-L-A-N-N
-E-D-O- B-S-O-L-E-S-C-

It is 6:30 A.M. and your body is startled by a voice reporting the war in
Iraq, a voice reporting the war in Iraq,
a voice reporting the war in Iraq, a
voice reporting the war in Iraq, a voice
reporting the war in Iraq, a voice
reporting the war in Iraq.

Your body reaches over, extending its
right arm and hand.

It reaches over to turn off the alarm
clock on the bed stand.

The right index finger of your body
pushes the stop button on the *Emerson
SmartSet* radio.

With its index finger and thumb your
body turns on the bedside lamp.

Your body turns on the lamp in this
way.

As the right leg of your body pushes
out from under the covers, the left leg
of your body follows as it sits up on
the side of the bed.

Your body's two feet are flat on the
cold floor now.

From a sitting position your body
stands and turns to the left.

With one foot in front of the other, it
walks around the bed.

On its way out of the bedroom, your body switches on the *Sony Trinitron to CNN*...

...listening to the latest casualties, Listening to the latest casualties, Listening to the latest casualties, Listening to the latest casualties, Listening to the latest casualties, it enters the bathroom.

> *Voice box (Vocom)*: Prefabricated implants are pushed against paralyzed vocal cords in the thyroid cartilage, which force them to tighten, restoring speech. (Harper, 2002, p. 54)

After doing so, your body switches on a bank of 6 incandescent lights.

Having illuminated itself your body stares into the large mirror examining itself.

Maneuvering a shiny metallic swivel handle, your body turns on the water faucet.

It fills the basin with warm water and with cupped hands it splashes itself.

While pressing on a pump, your body's right hand dispenses soap into its palm.

Bending its arm at the elbow, it raises the foamy substance to its face.

In an upward and downward motion its hands lather its facial parts.

It fills the basin with warm water and with cupped hands it splashes itself.

Next, with its electric toothbrush filled with *Colgate*, your body then cleans its teeth.

As the right hand of your body returns the toothbrush to its holder, its left hand reaches over and turns on the showerhead.

After the left leg of your body steps into the shower, your right leg follows.

As your body receives the gentle massage of the adjustable *WaterPik* showerhead, Wolf Blitzer's report of collateral damage, . . .

. . . report of collateral damage, report of collateral damage, report of collateral damage, report of collateral damage, report of collateral damage, report of collateral damage emanates from the bedroom television set.

> *Ear (Clarion II Bionic Ear)*: an external processor (worn behind the ear like a hearing aid) converts sounds into digital code, then transmits it to a cochlear implant. The acoustic nerve in the ear canal then interprets the signal as sound. (Harper, 2002, p. 54)

After drying itself, your body reaches for the *Kathie Lee 1600* to blow-dry its hair.

Your body can no longer hear the report from the high-pitched sound of the dryer.

Upon leaving the bathroom, your body turns off the lights and returns to the bedroom.

After dressing itself your body straps a *Timex* onto its wrist.

Using the tips of its index finger and thumb it adjusts the dial to the correct time.

Next, using its left hand your body picks up a pair of eyeglasses.

As the left hand holds them steady, your body's right hand wipes its lenses with *Kleenex*.

As one foot precedes the other, your body walks down the staircase to the kitchen.

It turns on the kitchen *Sony* to *CNN* only to catch suicide bombings in Baghdad,…

. . . suicide bombings in Baghdad, suicide bombings in Baghdad, suicide bombings in Baghdad, suicide bombings in Baghdad, suicide bombings in Baghdad, suicide bombings in Baghdad.

> *Eyes (smart eye band)*: A device (worn behind the ear) generates a magnetic field that activates the implanted muscle. The band, designed primarily for reading, can be switched on and off. (Harper, 2002, p. 54)

Opening the *Amana* refrigerator, your body pulls out a carton of processed orange juice with pulp.

After filling a glass, it downs a 1,000 ml. of vitamin C and a multiple vitamin pill.

It then fills the *Krups* coffee grinder with Sumatra Mendheling and presses on the switch.

As your body grinds the beans to a fine consistency the water comes to a boil.

The teapot whistling on the stove heard throughout the house penetrates its ears.

Your body's olfactory organ smells the freshly brewed coffee dripping into an insulated stainless steel *Thermos* mug.

It then places a small pitcher of cream into the *Kenmore* and microwaves its contents to lukewarm.

After pouring the cream into the coffee, your body gets a whiff from the electric bread maker.

Having filled it with ingredients the night before, it kneads and bakes automatically.

Its buzzer goes off telling your body it is time to take out the fresh loaf for breakfast.

The *Sunbeam* toaster requires your body to push down a lever after it places the slices in its slots.

Popping up after it is ready, the toasted bread is buttered for your body to eat.

As it is walking out the door to the *Plymouth Voyager*, your body hears Christiane Amanpour.

Her televised body tells your body about the day's body count, . . .

. . . about the day's body count, about the day's body count, about the day's body count, about the day's body count, about the day's body count, about the day's body count.

Eyes (Artificial silicon retinas): A microchip is inserted into the retina through a small incision. The chip converts light into electricity, restoring sight. (Harper, 2002, p. 54)

16 dead, 587 wounded, 34 missing, 12 POWs.

With the right index finger and thumb, your body inserts a key into the door lock.

Turning the key to the left enables your body to unlock the door and enter the vehicle.

It straps on a seat belt, inserts the key into the electronic ignition, and starts the 6-cylinder engine.

Its foot pressing on the throttle, your body revs up the engine to 4,000 RPMs.

After adjusting the rear and side mirrors, your body shifts the automatic transmission into reverse.

With its left hand on the steering wheel, it backs the *Voyager* out of the garage.

While doing so it turns on *NPR* to hear more on toppling the regime and nation building, . . .

. . . toppling the regime and nation building, toppling the regime and nation building, toppling the regime and nation building, toppling the regime and nation building, toppling the regime.

Heart (AbioCor heart): this titanium and plastic blood pump replaces the human heart. A battery belt worn around the

patient's midriff feeds electricity to the heart. To recharge,
the patient plugs into an AC outlet. (Harper, 2002, p. 54)

Having arrived at the traffic light,
your body pushes on the brakes with its
right foot.

As the *Voyager* comes to a halt, your
body turns on the windshield wipers.

Your body's eyes can now see the street
more clearly as it drives ahead.

The light turns green and your body
shifts its foot from the brakes to the
throttle.

At 3,500 RPMs it can hear the smooth
shifting of gears in the transmission.

Another red light and its foot presses
on the brakes only to change to throttle.

The light changes immediately upon
approach and your body has to quickly
adjust.

Its eyes keep shifting between one side
mirror to the next, and the rear mirror.

Traffic is heavy so your body feels
anxious as it maneuvers the *Voyager*.

Enroute to its destination, your body
witnesses a large construction crane
lifting heavy machinery.

As the load is gently lowered onto a
curvilinear building, your body senses
relief.

As if in response to this stimulus, it
turns the knob of the car radio with its
index finger and thumb.

It's Bob Edwards on *NPR's Morning Edition* reporting refugees caught in crossfire in Basra, . . .

. . . refugees caught in crossfire in Basra, refugees caught in crossfire in Basra, refugees caught in crossfire in Basra, refugees caught in crossfire in Basra, refugees caught in crossfire in Basra.

Nervous system (VNS therapy model 102 pulse generator): An electrode embedded in a nerve in the neck activates a generator every few seconds, preventing epileptic seizures and alleviating depression. (Harper, 2002, p. 54)

As your body steers the *Voyager* into the lot, its eyes search for parking.

Finding a spot, it pulls in, applies the brakes, and turns off the ignition.

With its left hand it opens the door and slides its legs out onto the pavement.

After it stands up, it turns around, grabs its briefcase, and shuts the door.

Inserting the key into the slot, it locks the door and begins to move away.

As it places one foot in front of the other, it walks toward its workplace.

A number of obstacles have to be negotiated to prevent collisions.

A tree, brick wall, several other bodies, a trashcan, and a fire hydrant are encountered.

Upon arriving at its destination, the right hand of your body pushes on a lever.

Opening the door, it enters the building and walks to a stairway.

There, it lifts one foot after the other to ascend to the second floor.

The hand of your body presses another lever to open yet another door.

Having entered the space of its office, it walks immediately to the *Macintosh G4*.

Its right hand grasps an electronic mouse and pushes a button to reboot.

Electronic e-mail is the first to appear on the screen reporting that Allies intensify air assault, . . .

. . . Allies intensify air assault, Allies intensify air assault, Allies intensify air assault, Allies intensify air assault, Allies intensify air assault, Allies intensify air assault.

> *Neurons (neurochips)*: Tiny microchips mimic the way neurons fire in the central nervous system. Intended to repair damage to the brain or spinal cord. (Harper, 2002, p. 54)

While reading the daily barrage of e-mail, your body hears the telephone ring.

After picking up, your body opens its mouth and speaks into the receiver.

Bla-laul-tualt-toulst-sowout-toud-toudk-tout-ruog-pout-pa, it speaks, speaks, and speaks.

Then suddenly it drops the receiver on its cradle and returns back to the screen in silence.

Another's body walks into your body's office and bends itself at the waist.

Lowering its buttocks, it sits in a chair, opens its mouth, shouting, demanding.

The other body's arms flail, its fingers point at yours, its face reddens.

Your body casually leans back in its high tech *Herman Miller* designer chair, and tilts its neck.

Looking upward it sees the four florescent light fixtures suspended from the ceiling.

One in particular captures your body's attention with the sounds of its buzzing ballast.

The eyes of your body focus on the greenish tint of the lights to escape the confrontation.

After 45 minutes have passed the other thrusts its body upward and stands upright.

It turns to its right and places one foot in front of the other and walks out the office.

As it does, your body's mind wanders, recalling the daily news reports while listening to the buzzing ballast, . . .

. . . listening to the buzzing ballast, listening to the buzzing ballast, listening to the buzzing ballast, listening to the buzzing ballast, listening to the buzzing ballast.

Arm (neural bypass robotic arm): Electrodes implanted in the cerebral cortex send neuron signals to a microprocessor in a wearable computer. It matches impulses to different arm movements. Once trained this system can drive a robotic arm. (Harper, 2002, p. 55)

. . . your body is startled by a voice reporting the war in Iraq, a voice report- ing the war in Iraq, a voice reporting the war in Iraq, a voice reporting the war in Iraq, a voice reporting the war in Iraq, a voice reporting the war in Iraq, a voice reporting the war in Iraq.

Left ventricle (Novacor): An electromechanical pump inserted into the abdominal wall pushes blood into the arter- ies. (Harper, 2002, p. 55)

. . . your body switches on the *Sony Trini- tron to CNN* . . . Listening to the latest casualties, Listening to the latest casu- alties, Listening to the latest casual- ties, Listening to the latest casualties, Listening to the latest casualties, Lis- tening to the latest casualties . . .

Liver (Bioreactor): An external bioreactor—essentially a portable dialysis machine made of plastic foam—removes toxins from the patient's blood. (Harper, 2002, p. 55)

. . . reports of collateral damage, reports of collateral damage, reports of collateral damage, reports of collateral damage, reports of collateral damage, reports of collateral damage, reports of collateral damage, reports of collateral damage, reports of collateral damage . . .

Hand (Dextra): Sensors in the artificial hand respond to electrical signals from the arm muscles and tendons. The signals are transmitted to a belt-mounted computer that controls fingers individually. (Harper, 2002, p. 55)

. . . only to catch suicide bombings in Baghdad, suicide bombings in Baghdad, suicide bombings in Baghdad, suicide bombings in Baghdad, suicide bombings in Baghdad, suicide bombings in Baghdad, suicide bombings in Baghdad . . .

Joints (Giolite knee): A friction-controlled polycentric device is inserted into the joint socket. Its plastic cup works with a metal ball and stem to flex up to 20 degrees. (Harper, 2002, p. 55)

. . . her body tells your body about the day's body count, about the day's body count, about the day's body count, about the day's body count, about the day's body count, about the day's body count, about the day's body count . . .

Nerves and muscles (Bion): Radio-powered implant stimulates nerves and muscles, restoring movement to paralyzed limbs. (Harper, 2002, p. 55)

. . . to hear more on toppling the regime and nation building, toppling the regime and nation building, toppling the regime and nation building, toppling the regime and nation building, toppling the regime and nation building, toppling the regime.

Muscle (artificial muscles): These muscles expand and contract as the stuff they're made of, polypyrrole, generates and conducts electricity. (Harper, 2002, p. 55)

. . . refugees caught in crossfire in Basra, refugees caught in crossfire in

Basra,   refugees   caught   in   crossfire   in
Basra,   refugees   caught   in   crossfire   in
Basra,   refugees   caught   in   crossfire   in
Basra,   refugees   caught   in   crossfire   in
Basra.

> *Leg (C-Leg)*: Sensors in the knee and the shin react to movement and weight distribution up to 50 times per second, adjusting the leg's position accordingly. (Harper, 2002, p. 55)

...that Allies intensify air assault,
Allies intensify air assault, Allies
intensify air assault, Allies intensify
air   assault,   Allies   intensify   air
assault, Allies intensify air assault,
Allies intensify air assault, Allies
intensify air assault, Allies intensify
air assault.

> *Bone (Vitoss)*: Synthetic materials, such as calcium phosphate, replace the marrow, stimulating new bone growth. Helpful in bone-grafting operations. (Harper, 2002, p. 55)

...your body's mind wanders to the daily
news   reports   while   listening   to   the
buzzing ballast, listening to the buzzing
ballast, listening to the buzzing ballast, listening to the buzzing ballast,
listening to the buzzing ballast, listening to the buzzing ballast.

> *Cells (Bionic chip)*: A microchip regulates the activity of healthy human cells to more effectively administer gene therapy. An external wireless device sends the body's electrical impulses to the chip, which triggers the cells' membrane pores to open. (Harper, 2002, p. 55)

The *Oxford English Dictionary* defines
planned obsolescence as the "obsolescence of manufactured goods due to

deliberate changes in design, cessation of the supply of spare parts, use of poor-quality materials, etc."

In a chilling article in a recent issue of *Wired* magazine (March 2003) science reporter Jennifer Kahn writes about human bodies being used to store human organs. The body is technology is the body. Kahn describes a:

> ...dead man's room, [where] a different calculus is unfolding. Here the organ is the patient, and the patient is a mere container, the safest place to store body parts until surgeons are ready to use them. It can be more than a day from the time a donor dies until his organs are harvested—the surgery alone takes hours, not to mention the time needed to do blood tests, match tissue, and fly in special surgical teams for the evisceration. And yet, a heart lasts at most six hours outside the body, even after it has been kneaded, flushed with preservatives, and packed in a cooler. Organs left on ice too long tend to perform poorly in their new environment, and doctors are picky about which viscera they're willing to work with. Even an ailing cadaver is a better container than a cooler. (Kahn, 2003, pp. 132-137)

The body is technology is the body is technology is the body is technology is the body...

```
P-L-A-N-N-E-D-O-B-S-O-L-E-S-C-E-N-C-E-
P-L-A-N-N-E-D-O-B-S-O-L-E-S-C-E-N-C-E-
P-L-A-N-N-E-D-O-B-S-O-L-E-S-C-E-N-C-E-P
-L-A-N-N-E-D-O-B-S-O-L-E-S-C-E-N-C-E-P-
L-A-N-N-E-D-O-B-S-O-L-E-S-C-E-N-C-E-P-
L-A-N-N-E-D-O-B-S-O-L-E-S-C-E-N-C-E-P-L
-A-N-N-E-D-O-B-S-O-L-E-S-C-E-N-C-E-P-L-
A-N-N-E-D-O-B-S-O-L-E-S-C-E-N-C-E-P-L-
A-N-N-E-D-O-B-S-O-L-E-S-C-E-N-C-E-
```

. . . reporting   the   war   in
Iraq . . . listening to the latest casualties . . . reports   of   collateral
damage . . . suicide   bombings   in   Baghdad . . . about   the   day's   body
count . . . the toppling of the regime and
nation building . . . refugees caught in
crossfire in Basra . . . Allies intensify
air assault, . . .

. . . *bla-laul-tualt-toulst-sowout-toud-
toudk-tout-ruog-pout-pa,* it   speaks,
speaks, and speaks . . .

The Spectacle of Visual Culture

> In a society dominated by the production and consumption of images, no part of life can remain immune from the invasion of spectacle.
>
> —Christopher Lasch, 1991, p. 122

> The spectacle is the acme of ideology, for in its full flower it exposes and manifests the essence of all ideological systems: the impoverishment, enslavement and negation of real life.
>
> —Guy Debord, 1994, p. 151

Given the pervasive domination of society by visual culture through television, movies, the Internet, advertising, and other forms corporate production, the field of art education is currently in the process of defining curricular and pedagogical practices that will enable students to expose, examine, and critique the essentialized and immutable codes of mass mediated delivery systems. Is the critique of visual culture by art educators a legitimized form of voyeurism? Does the desire to covet its pleasures represent a form of cultural narcissism? What distinguishes between pleasure and criticism in the study of visual culture in art education?

This essay was initially presented at the National Art Education Association Annual Convention in Denver, Colorado, in April 2004 and later published in Summer 2004 by the National Art Education Association in *Studies in Art Education: A Journal of Issues and Research in Art Education*, 45(4) 298–312. It is reprinted from *Studies in Art Education: A Journal of Issues and Research in Art Education*, with permission from the National Art Education Association, 2004, www.naea-reston.org.

Although visual culture is well established (Chapman, 2003; Freedman, 2003; Kindler, 2003; Tavin, 2003; Wilson, 2003), in this essay we address these questions by conceptualizing visual culture as *spectacle pedagogy*. Spectacle, according to cultural critic Guy Debord (1994), "is not a collection of images; rather, it is a social relationship between people that is mediated by images" (p. 12). Or, as critical theorist Douglas Crimp explains, "an image isn't simple negative or positive but rather is the product of social relations and produces contradictory social effects" (Takemoto, 2003, p. 85). As visual pronouncements, images are ideological, they teach us what and how to see and think. They influence our choices and how we interact with one another. Considering this influence, we internalize the spectacle pedagogy of visual culture as naturalized dispositions in the body. In doing so, we constitute our identities as "one dimensional," according to cultural critic Herbert Marcuse. Bereft of criticality, one-dimensional thought is "populated by self-validating hypotheses which, incessantly and monopolistically repeated, become hypnotic definitions or dictations" (Marcuse, 1972, pp. 24–25).

We characterize the spectacle pedagogy of visual culture in two opposing ways: first, as a ubiquitous form of representation, which constitutes the pedagogical objectives of mass mediated culture and corporate capitalism to manufacture our desires and determine our choices; and second, as a democratic form of practice that enables a critical examination of visual cultural codes and ideologies to resist social injustice. As the former spectacle pedagogy functions as an insidious, ever-present form of propaganda in the service of cultural imperialism, the latter represents critical citizenship, which aspires toward cultural democracy. To resist the monocular regime of spectacle seduction, historian Martin Jay (1988) suggests a plurality of vision to "wean ourselves from the fiction of a 'true' [dominant cultural] vision and revel instead in the possibilities opened up by the scopic regimes we have already invented and the ones, now so hard to envision, that are doubtless to come" (p. 20).

A plurality of vision provides a framework for an inclusive democracy that has the possibility of yielding multiple perspectives, discourses, and understandings about cultural life. Short of such plurality, the undeniable lure of cultural spectacle becomes a form of narcissistic pathology. The current rise in private and public forms of surveillance through mass mediation supports this understanding of our desires to be consumed *by* and *in* images. As cultural critic bell hooks (1996, p. 2) suggests, some of us consume visual culture to be entertained and others seek it out to learn something. Even though visual culture in both these cases functions pedagogically, we argue that it is in our desire to learn something from it that we are constituted as critical spectators.

The Manufacture of Spectacle

Cultural critic Siegfried Kracauer (1963/1995) conceptualized the spectacle of visual culture as "the mass ornament," a metaphor he used to typify the ornamental patterns of the Tiller Girls, a synchronized dancing group in the 1920s, and equated their synchronized legs with factory workers' hands. By comparing the "capitalist production process" with that of "the mass ornament," he distinguished each of them as an "end in itself" (pp. 76, 78). Although ignorant of the obvious gender stereotypes embedded in his choice of metaphor, Kracauer's comparison of the performers and spectators of the mass ornament to workers used like component parts in a mechanized division of labor in modern factories corresponded with the rational plan of Taylorism (p. 78). He states, "The *ratio* that gives rise to the ornament [spectacle] is strong enough to invoke the mass and to expunge all life from the figures constituting it.... It is the *rational and empty form* of the cult, devoid of any explicit meaning, that appears in the mass ornament" (p. 84). Thus for Kracauer, as the insidious spectacle of visual culture constructs its constituent/component performers and spectators, it mutes their private, individual values, meanings, and desires for the good of the mass ornament.

Although Kracauer and the cultural critics of the Frankfurt School, namely Walter Benjamin and Theodor Adorno, wrote about the mechanized body of the mass ornament in the 1920s, later theorists such as economist Kenneth E. Boulding in the mid-1950s, and the historian Daniel J. Boorstin and media theorist Marshall McLuhan in the early 1960s, described what they were experiencing as the growing social, political, and economic effects of mass mediated images. These scholars explained our propensity to conceptualize and represent the reality of cultural life in images as a disposition that is epistemologically grounded. For Boulding (1961), beginning with the invention of writing to contemporary forms of imaging, the dynamics of a society is predicated on the assumption that "the image [as a 'dissociated transcript'] not only makes society, society continually remakes the image" (pp. 64–65).

Boorstin (1987) describes the same dynamic as "pseudo-events spawn[ing] other pseudo-events in geometric progression" (p. 33). "Pseudo-event" is Boorstin's designation for the spectacle of visual culture, which is the creation and dissemination of mass mediated images of cultural experience whose truths, realities, and meanings are complicated with ambiguity to arouse and captivate public interest (pp. 11, 35). Boorstin's notion of the pseudo-event corresponds with Adorno's earlier characterization of the "pseudo-personalization," which denotes the commodity fetishism created by the spectacle "culture industry" of capitalism (Adorno, 1991, p. 173). For McLuhan (1964), electronic media served as an organic extension of the body's nervous system, namely its instantaneous and simultaneous electric communications capability that manifests the body's "passive" rather than "active" experience (McLuhan, p. 219; Boorstin, p. 188). Thus, by extension, systems of electronic delivery such as the television, the computer, and the Internet are organically linked to the body, as McLuhan suggests, hence enabling an experience of their digitized visual culture that is paradoxically vicarious yet impelling as its ever-present images construct and determine our bodies' choices and desires.

Given its mass appeal, the power of spectacle culture is in its pedagogical functioning. Its captivating visual stimulus overwhelms and arrests our bodies' attention and in doing so inscribes it with the self-validating ideology of commodity culture, a form of "titillation" that journalist Lawrence Weschler refers to as "Pavlovian" (Bernhard, 1998, Electronic version). With its persistent indoctrination and commodification of our bodies, spectacle culture continues to establish itself as a driving force in determining both private and public desires, which media critics Edward S. Herman and Noam Chomsky (1988) refer to as the "manufacture of consent." Significant about their characterization of the power of the media is its paradoxical pedagogy of "debate, criticism, and dissent," which unlike that of radical democratic practice enables and perpetuates the commodity culture of corporate capitalism (p. 302).

This "politics as spectacle," as cultural critic Christopher Lasch (1991) has labeled it, represents a form of propaganda that "create[s] in the public a chronic sense of crisis, which in turn justifies the expansion of executive power and the secrecy surrounding it" (p. 78). Political historian Timothy Mitchell (1998) claims that this dominant order of criticality represents the "world-as-exhibition" where citizens are "continually pressed into service as [complacent] spectators" (p. 298). As such the critique that yields the world-as-exhibition by Madison Avenue advertising and other forms of mass mediation manufactures our "narcissus fixation" with this cultural spectacle, which occludes our critical understanding of its content as commodity fetishism (McLuhan, 1964, p. 33; Marcuse, 1972, p. 25; Lasch, 1991, p. 47).

Art educator Neil C. M. Brown (2003) raises similar concerns about the paradox of "advocating" and "elevating" popular culture, "under the banner of Cultural Studies, to a state of 'seriousness' commensurable with the high arts" (p. 286). Such advocacy for visual culture studies can very well replicate the authorized transgressions of corporate capitalism while ignoring the potential of visual culture to resist social injustice. The danger of *focusing* on the critical deconstruction of visual culture as an end in itself is an immanent one that leads to an "ethical cynicism that provides no guarantees for social reconstruction in the practice of art education," argues Brown (p. 288).

In effect, what appears as transgressive pedagogy may not always be the case claims cultural historian Elizabeth Wilson:

> We transgress in order to insist that we are, that we exist, and to place a distance between ourselves and the dominant culture. But we have to go further—we have to have an idea of how things could be different, otherwise transgression is mere [narcissistic] posturing. In other words, transgression on its own leads eventually to entropy, unless we carry within us some idea of transformation. It is therefore not

transgression that should be our watchword, but transformation. (Quoted in hooks, 1996, p. 26)

Given that contemporary cultural life is always already
immersed in spectacle, we affirm the necessity for a broad and
inclusive understanding of visual cultural studies through a "plurality of scopic regimes," which includes the transgressive and
transformative power of art making. Indeed, for the purposes of
art education curriculum and pedagogy, this inclusive understanding is imperative.

The Spectacle of Politics and
the Politics of Spectacle

Well, you weren't surprised were you? Did you expect anything
less spectacular from Mr. Universe-turned-*Conan the Barbarian*-
turned-*Terminator*-turned-*Kindergarten Cop*-turned-movie star-
turned-businessman-turned-multimillionaire-turned governor?
Muscle man Arnold Schwarzenegger has done it yet again,
reinvented himself as he staged a last-minute, all-out campaign
to recall and replace incumbent Governor Gray Davis in the
circuslike climate of the October 2003 California gubernatorial
race. With no previous government experience, his only claim to
the national political scene was having strategically married into
the Kennedy clan. Only fate would have it that this union of the
political right and left would yield a viable candidate in the
future. In true Hollywood movie-making fashion, "Arnold" has
always understood the visual hyperbole and power of the spectacle to turn people's heads, to fix their gaze, to command attention, to use his own vanity to mirror the public's narcissistic
desires. As Boorstin (1987) suggests, as a human pseudo-event, a
"celebrity [such as Schwarzenegger] is a person who is known for
his [or her] well-knownness" (p. 57).

Banking on Schwarzenegger's larger-than-life persona, the
myth of his filmic characters, "his well-knownness," his highly
publicized campaign influenced not only a large voter turn out,
but he also won at the polls by an unexpected, overwhelming
margin. Whether referring to his constituents as "viewers" during

his campaign or being referred to by them as having the makings of a "strong governor" because of his body's behemoth bulk, he successfully marketed himself by using his star appeal to gain the support of the voters.

Backed by a team of wealthy, high-profile business, media, and political strategists, Schwarzenegger's campaign was quickly, albeit carefully, orchestrated with just the right amount of words, the right amount of interviews, the right amount of debates, the right amount of commercial time, and the right amount of dollars, all of which ironically corresponds with cultural critic Susan Sontag's (1977, p. 180) polemical appeal for an "ecology of images"—not to mention an ecology of gubernatorial candidates given the field of 135 nominees—albeit with a capitalist twist. This campaign was a case where not knowing what to say, not wanting to say anything, and not knowing how to debate ironically worked in the candidate's favor.

Apropos Schwarzenegger's awesome spectacle in the California political scene, literary critic Roland Barthes (1977) characterized the snare of the photographic image in the electoral myth making process as follows. "Inasmuch as photography is an ellipse of language and a condensation of an 'ineffable' social whole, it constitutes an anti-intellectual weapon and tends to spirit away 'politics' (that is to say a body of problems and solutions) to the advantage of a 'manner of being', a socio-moral status" (p. 91). Indeed, Barthes, Boorstin (1987, p. 61), and literary critic Louis Menand (2004, p. 84) argue that the mirror of photography, which can also be attributed to television and visual culture in general, enables a narcissistic complicity whereby political candidates and their voters find likenesses in each other. As the candidate is exalted through her or his photogenic qualities, "the voter is at once expressed and heroized, he [or she] is invited to elect himself [or herself], to weigh the mandate which he [or she] is about to give with a veritable physical transference" (Barthes, 1977, p. 92). Thus, similar to the objectifying gaze of psychologist Jacques Lacan's mirror (1977, pp. 1–2), Schwarzenegger's constituency bestows him and is in turn bestowed with mythic power. This relinquishment of reality to myth "depoliticizes speech," argues Barthes, and in doing so myth empties reality of its history and naturalizes its historical insignificance (pp.

142–143). For philosopher Richard Rorty (1979) the philosophical idea of such a self-referential epistemology, which assumes that knowledge mirrors the world in the form of mythic representations, must be continually challenged with the critical pragmatism of cultural history and politics.

According to journalist Andrew Sullivan (2003), Arnold represents a "new kind of politician." "In our political wars, he's a synthesis. In our culture wars, he's a truce," qualities that Sullivan attributes to Arnold's blend of fiscal conservatism and social liberalism (p. 88). "[Arnold] was one of the first major movie stars who winked at the audience, understanding that they too were intelligent enough to see through the pyrotechnics and absurd dialogue to be amused by the pure entertainment of the spectacle" (p. 88). Indeed, the 1993 film *Last Action Hero* corroborates the irony of Schwarzenegger's wink. A depiction of "blockbuster mentality and movie fan obsession... [the film] clearly plays to an ironically intertextual mode of address as the film within a film simultaneously plays to and satirizes the high-octane Schwarzenegger star vehicle," explains film critic Rebecca D. Feasey (n.d., Electronic version). What Sullivan and Feasey have identified in Arnold is a shrewd man whose identity is constructed by and for the media.

Given his essentialized position within the culture, is Schwarzenegger's mixture of right and left politics trustworthy? Considering his clever use of irony in his films, does the parody of his "wink" serve as a critical gesture to entertain and perpetuate institutionalized and corporate politics, or does it serve as a genuine disruption to resist social injustice? Art educator jan jagodzinski (2003) believes it is the former. He asserts that while Hollywood's wink lets the audience "know that what they are watching is simply exaggerated artifice," it nonetheless creates the "false consciousness" [in the Marxian sense] of the "capitalist subject" that outwardly resists corporate capitalism while believing in its myth on the inside (pp. 108–109). Likewise, literary critic Linda Hucheon (1985) suggests that the parody of the Hollywood wink, while appearing subversive, in actuality is an "authorized transgression" (p. 26), "authorized by the very norm it seeks to subvert. Even in mocking, parody reinforces; in formal terms, it inscribes the mocked conventions onto itself, thereby guaranteeing their continued existence" (p. 75).

Insofar as the mass media demands viewers' loyalty to the spectacle of visual culture, it constructs their identities as "fanatics," or in the more innocuous and acceptable use of the word as "fans." Sociologist Pierre Bourdieu (1990) explains that such objectification of everyday life "constitutes the social world as a spectacle offered to an observer who takes up a 'point of view' on the action and who, putting into the object the principles of his relation to the object, proceeds as if it were intended solely for knowledge and as if all the interactions within it were purely symbolic exchanges" (p. 52). Although poet, critic, and philosopher Samuel Taylor Coleridge (1817/1985) long ago suggested experiencing spectacular symbolic exchanges through "the willing suspension of disbelief for the moment that constitutes poetic faith," such willingness to surrender one's critical faculties is vulnerable to being consumed, co-opted by the commodity motives of visual culture claims Debord (1994).

Debord's manifesto-like aphorisms in *The Society of the Spectacle* (1994) were written "with the deliberate intention of doing harm to spectacular society" (p. 10). They represent his vigilant positioning to expose, examine, and critique the acculturation of socially and historically constructed symbolic representations and dispositions of spectacle culture, the *habitus* against which Bourdieu (1990) suggests one has to "situate oneself within 'real activity'...the preoccupied, active presence in the world through which the world imposes its presence, with its urgencies" (p. 52). Bourdieu's concept of the "real" is not that of reality TV where fame-seeking contestants are paid to perform bizarre, and often emotionally and physically dangerous feats, on television shows such as *Survivor, Dog Eat Dog, Fear Factor*, and *The Bachelor,* to confront the reality of their individual fears.

The trivialized notion of "challenge" on these shows represents an extreme example of commodity fetishism, an insatiable appetite for gazing at others, who, while serving as our surrogates, undertake ridiculous risks for our pleasure and our hope of attaining sublime levels of personal experience, albeit vicariously, while we sit complacently in the comfort and safety of our living rooms. For jagodzinski (2003) the desire for such vicarious thrills valorizes the "*jouissance,*" the "pleasure of resistance" and in doing so creates the fertile conditions of late capitalism, by constituting "subversive and destabilized [multiple and fluid] identities who seek new modes of enjoyment through forms of romanticized resistances" (pp. 107, 115).[1] For Bourdieu (1990), such pleasured, internalized dispositions and idealisms of the social world impelled by visual culture, *habitus*, represents a social reality that is consistent with Barthes's (1977) characterization of mythic power, which "depoliticizes critical speech."

Cultural critic Jean Baudrillard (1994) concurs as he explains that the unidirectional gaze of the Panopticon is no longer a fitting metaphor for television. Given that its simulations now precede reality, we "no longer watch TV, it is TV that watches [us] (live)" (p. 29). The paradoxical crisis of reality TV, its enabling of "being there without being there," abolishes participatory citizenship as it blurs the distinction between viewers' passive and active involvement in society and, in doing so, purges society of its political dimension (pp. 22–30). To challenge such complacent dispositions, Barthes (1991, p. 119) calls for a response to images that probes beyond the conformity of the spectacle and into an "ecstatic," embodied depth of being where the self cannot be tamed. It is within such an embodied depth, we argue, that we can find a space for transformation.

In his prescient essay "Cult of Distraction," cultural critic Siegfried Kracauer (1963/1995) echoes Barthes's imperative for confronting the "empirical habits" of photographic spectacle. Kracauer makes a case for the importance of exposing, examining, and critiquing "the mass ornament" to resist the regressive politics of historicism, the assumption that history is coherently constructed. Insofar as "distraction" exposes the complex and contradictory circumstances of contemporary cultural life it ruptures and makes possible a critical turn in the apparent flow of history. Thus, the *disclosure* of the spectacle of visual culture is morally and ethically significant, according to Kracauer, because it enables a critique of its mass mediated codes and delivery systems (p. 326). If the potential for its critique is not realized, the distraction of spectacle culture becomes transgressive unto itself as it takes on a cult status that results in the self-indulgent, voyeuristic culture of narcissism (p. 326).

Visual Culture and Its Encounter with Art

Not uncoincidentially, the media of collage, montage, assemblage, installation, and performance—arguably five of the most significant contributions of the twentieth century to the history of art—emerged during a century of mass mediated production.[2] Visual artists beginning with the Cubists, Futurists, Dadaists, and Constructivists at the beginning of the century through to the performance and installation artists of the 1980s and 1990s understood the power of visual culture and the need to contextualize the allure of its spectacle within art to problematize the authority of its capitalist ideology. Such exploration and improvisation of new images, ideas, and utopian representations are critical for the survival of subjectivity in contemporary times. Although the multicentric representations of artists who used these media suggested early signs of postmodernity during the early 1900s, these artists nevertheless retained the political and aesthetic objectives of the Modernist patriarchy until the late 1960s and early 1970s. During the civil rights movement, the feminist movement, and the anti-war demonstrations of the Vietnam War, these modes of representation were fully reconstituted as agonistic strategies in the service of postmodern identity politics.

Since then contemporary artists such as Rachel Rosenthal, Barbara Kruger, Cindy Sherman, David Wojnarowicz, Guillermo Gómez-Peña, the Guerrilla Girls, and others have used these media's liminal, contingent, and ephemeral strategies to challenge social and political injustice. Given the feminist slogan, "the personal is political," they focused on performances of subjectivity, through transgressive artistic acts constructed from private memory and cultural history that in the face of dominant politics of public, institutionalized culture represent social activism in the arts. Some of the most provocative of these performances are those that are "site-specific," occurring within the very public places of dominant culture. Krzysztof Wodiczko, a Polish-born contemporary artist who spent the first half of his life in the Soviet Union and now resides in Canada and the United States, is one such contemporary artist whose public, site-specific, multimedia performances in international politically charged hot spots are aimed at enabling a public discourse on cultural oppression. Wodiczko explains, "Public space is a site of enactment. It belongs to no one, yet we all are a part of it and can bring meaning to it" (quoted in Phillips, 2003, p. 35). Having lived in a closed, oppressive society, Wodiczko's objective with public art is the attainment of cultural democracy through critical citizenship.

An artist who uses the strategies of collage, montage, assemblage, installation, and performance art interchangeably, Wodiczko believes in intervening and challenging the oppressive cultural forces that determine our choices, desires, and uses of new and emerging technologies.

His recent performance in the United States, *The Mouthpiece* (2003), consisted of outfitting aliens, residents and nonresidents, legal and illegal immigrants, with an electronic audiovisual recording "instrument," worn over the mouth ironically like a gag, to speak out in public spaces where they are ordinarily silenced and perceived invisible. The wearer of the instrument is able to prerecord a video image and audio voice of his or her mouth in the act of speaking and to replay and reperform it in a time and space of their choosing. Such work echoes poet Audre Lorde's (1984) call for the use of language to transform silence into action. Lorde recognizes that we might stay silent for many reasons, including "fear of contempt, of censure, or some judgment, or recognition, of challenge, or annihilation. But most of all, I think, we fear the visibility without which we cannot truly live" (p. 42). What both Lorde and Wodiczko have realized is that without finding a means through which we can speak, transformation is impossible.

Considering the spectacles of racial profiling, "zero tolerance" at the U.S. borders, and the general hysteria over international terrorism, which have raised suspicions about and silenced the Other since the 9/11 attacks, this and other Wodiczko works serve as poignant metaphors in speaking to, challenging, and resisting the mass media's globalization of xenophobia. For Wodiczko (n.d.), *The Mouthpiece* serves as "democratic artifice," one that:

> points to the absurdity of any attempt at depriving speech rights in a democratic society. It responds to the actual political process and experience of such deprivation, while at the

Figure 2.1. Krzysztof Wodiczko, *The Mouthpiece*, 2003. Courtesy Galerie Lelong, New York, NY.

same time it helps to translate this disadvantage into a new advantage. In other words, it is an instrument whose function is to empower those who are deprived of power. (Wodiczko, Electronic version).

Similar to his other public performances, Wodiczko's situates the body in a "live, performance assemblage" composed of heterogeneous, independent remnants of visual, electronic culture. In the spirit of philosophers Gilles Deleuze and Félix Guattari (1987), the body in Wodiczko's work serves as a "desiring machine" as it "deterritorializes" stereotypical representations of mass mediated culture as component parts and "reterritorializes" them within the context of art to create new knowledge and unforeseen visual and conceptual machinations (pp. 54–55). By considering the body as a component part in this way, Wodiczko "grafts" its materiality with that of other remnants, electronic devices in the case of The Mouthpiece, each serving as a "prosthetic" to enable the body to perform its subjectivity against the grain of dominant cultural politics. Thus the contingent space of assemblage and performance art represents a public agonistic site for Wodiczko, where the oppressed can participate in cultural politics in active rather than passive ways by "step[ping] out of their communities, to engage in independent speech. When they return [to their communities] it is with a form of agency and insight" (Phillips, 2003, p. 42).

The underlying principle of collage, montage, assemblage, installation, and performance art is its disjunctive, segmented, and often-disparate representations of visual forms. As such, these media represent acts of perception as disjunctive associations between and among cultural experiences—dissociations, which enable spectators to participate in the creation of meaningful yet mutable conjunctions. The dissociations of these media assume that all human experience is disjunctive, a problematic epistemology that requires creative conjunctions to enable new and differentiated understandings. These media cite and site visual culture within the context of art and, in doing so, serve as powerful metaphors of how the phenomenon of visual culture is always already constituted as disjunctive within society.

The Undecidable Pedagogy of Art Making

The potential of collage, montage, assemblage, installation, and performance art as critical pedagogy for visual culture in art education lies in their dissonant spaces, at the contested borders that exist between their dissociative remnants. Such "in-between" spaces for media and education critic Elizabeth Ellsworth (1997) are conceptually and emotionally charged. Their "volatility" is caused by the "imperfect fits" among the remnants of mass mediated culture found in these art forms (pp. 38–39). Citing cultural critic Shoshanna Felman's (1987) writing about Freudian and Lacanian psychoanalytic pedagogy, Ellsworth argues that the slippage and indeterminacy of knowledge that occurs within these volatile spaces creates an errant, "undecidable" condition where meaning is continually negotiated and teaching as position of absolute authority is rendered "impossible."

Using the medium of film as a pedagogical metaphor, Ellsworth (1997) claims visual culture is constituted by its "mode of address," the means by which the mass media assumes to know who its audience is and what it desires. Based on these assumptions, the objectives of the mass media are to construct audience members' subject positions as consumers of visual culture. Nevertheless, Ellsworth argues that the imperfect fits between the mode of address in visual culture and viewers' responses and therefore makes it "possible to see the address of a text [or image or both] as a powerful, yet paradoxical, event whose power comes from the *difference* [undecidability] between address and response" (p. 37). Concerning critical pedagogy, Ellsworth asks an important question about the undecidability enabled by the paradoxical mode of address of visual culture. "What might a teacher make of the eventful and volatile space of difference or 'misfit' between who a curriculum thinks its students are or should be [their subject positions] and how students should actually use a curriculum's [mode of] address to constitute themselves and to act on and within history" (p. 37)? Thus, given the misfits between students' and the teacher's curriculum, Ellsworth argues that the pedagogical challenge is not one of transgression but transformation.

Ellsworth's theory of impossibility is good news for critical art educators given that it opens a dialogic space within which to critique the spectacle apparatus of visual culture. Her concept of "imperfect fits" corresponds with the disjunctive, paradoxical association between academic school curricula and students' personal memories and cultural histories. Given that students are always already immersed in visual culture, their personal experiences and perspectives serve as "montage" remnants within the classroom, differing modes of address that provide opportunities for their critical intervention and transformation. As a pedagogical metaphor the undecidable conditions that are created by the imperfect mode of address of visual culture and students' performances of subjectivity enables them to learn about and challenge the commodity fetishism of the spectacle of visual culture.

The slippage and undecidability of meaning that occurs in Ellsworth's in-between spaces is consistent with cultural critic Michel Foucault's (1972) "enunciative function," a mutability that enables language to resist and transgress the boundaries of codified culture. According to Foucault, the enunciative function ensures such slippage through the complexity and contradiction of language (p. 105). It is within the gaps that separate the specific, paradoxical, and multivocal conditions of the enunciative function that transgressive and transformative representations and interpretations are possible. As such, the infinite potential of the enunciative function of language represents for Foucault "archaeology of knowledge," whereby socially and historically codified representations are "excavated," examined and critiqued (p. 206).

Using the strategies of collage, montage, assemblage, installation, and performance art, contemporary artists' create volatile spaces within their artwork to evoke the enunciative function. In doing so, cultural critic Carol Becker (2002) claims they "assume the role of 'immanent critique,' in a dialectical sense, which is to say that instead of offering superficial solutions, they expose society's inherent contradictions; and instead of pursuing absolute truths, they offer complexity, ambivalence, and, at times, aggressive confrontations with the status quo" (p. 17). The critical strategies enabled through collage, montage, assemblage, installation, and performance art suggest that these media represent a significant means through which art students can learn to create immanent critiques of the spectacle of visual culture through art making.

To avoid misunderstanding, we are not limiting the concept of immanent critique merely to students' collage, montage, assemblage, installation, and performance art projects in the classroom. Rather, we are suggesting that these modes of address have broader implications for challenging the dominant codes of contemporary cultural life given their volatile in-between spaces, which are constituted by the disparate, dissociative remnants of mass mediated culture. Considering that the postmodern condition is pervasively mediated by visual culture, our awareness of its dominating assumptions, and our ability to expose, examine, and critique its spectacle, make the critical pedagogy of collage, montage, assemblage, installation, and performance art all the more imperative.

Hence, the specific use of these art media for student assignments notwithstanding, all creative activities, be they in the art classroom, the school in general, or the culture at large, present the possibility for cultural resistance if understood as immanent critiques. Assuming that to be the case, these classroom art-making activities immanently qualify as examples of Kracauer's concept of critical "distraction," Barthes' "photographic ecstasy," McLuhan's and Lasch's critique of "narcissus fixation," and Ellsworth's "pedagogy of volatile spaces" assuming that students are presented with opportunities to understand the critical and paradoxical relationship between their art-making activities and the academic dispositions, the *habitus* of institutionalized schooling, and between the images and ideas that they create through art and the sensationalized pedagogy of the spectacle of visual culture. Therein lies the potential of art making for transgressive and transformative experiences in visual culture.

The Impossible Task as Ecological Imperative

Spectacle...is the opposite of dialogue.
            —Guy Debord, 1994, p. 17

On Tuesday, September 11, 2001, "ecological devastation" of unprecedented proportions was unleashed on the United States, in "our own backyard." Two United Airlines Boeing 767 jetliners with passengers and crew aboard en route from Boston to Los Angeles were hijacked and crashed into the Twin Towers of the World Trade Center in New York City. A third hijacked flight, an American Airlines Boeing 757 jetliner with passengers and crew en route from Dulles Airport in Washington, D.C., to Los Angeles, was taken down and blasted into the Pentagon. The terrorists who perpetrated these deplorable acts targeted the symbols of U.S. financial and military supremacy and apparently were aiming either for the White House or the U.S. Capitol with a fourth hijacking. After learning of the devastation in New York via cell phones, crew members and passengers aboard a United Airlines Boeing 757 jetliner on its way from Newark, N.J. to San Francisco, fought heroically with terrorists and forced the jetliner down in an empty field in Sommerset County southeast of Pittsburgh, Pennsylvania.

Given that this essay is about the impossible, enigmatic, and interventionist strategies of the Chicago-based performance art collective Goat Island and the critique of ecological devastation contained in their performance *The Sea & Poison,* we could not in good conscience proceed without linking Goat Island's work to the events of 9/11. Overwhelmed by these major calamities, we could not resist reading and hyperbolizing everything in our daily experiences, including the ideas for this essay, through the images that we witnessed in the mass media. The more overwhelmed we became, the more it overtook our writing to the point that the impossibilities, the enigma of these tragic events disrupted this essay.

Each of these despicable incidents, parts of a diabolical suicide mission carried out by al-Qaeda, an international terrorist network led by the exiled Saudi militant leader Osama Bin Laden hiding in Afghanistan, resulted in untold billions of dollars of destruction to property and thousands of lives being lost. Moreover, left behind in the wake of this disaster was the detritus of terrorism, or what cultural critic Andrew Ross (1994) refers to as "ecoterrorism" in characterizing the unprecedented magnitude of ecological destruction that resulted from the Gulf War just a decade earlier (p. 326). The immediate sites of devastation contained human and nonhuman debris, garbage, spilled toxic chemicals, and spewed toxic gases into the atmosphere. One estimate claimed 60 billion tons of debris came from the collapsed Twin Towers alone. What is difficult to ascertain at the time of this writing, however, are the long-term residual effects, those which in all probability will extend and permeate our nation and the world as both human and nonhuman resources are called on to clean, dispose, and rebuild what was destroyed.

Considering our collective obsession with the spectacle of the mass media, the terrorists and their cohorts understood the power of images. Greatly aware of our high-tech prowess and superpower status, they commandeered and used our most sophisticated aeronautic and surveillance technologies against us. An insidious form of "fallout," the mass media's around-the-clock blitz of images transmitted the news of this ecoterrorism worldwide, often trivializing and diminishing its ensuing tragedy. Considering the magnitude of our shock, fear, and anger over these events, the mass media force-fed and reinforced our collective desire for retaliation and retribution regardless of the consequences, including the racial profiling and abuse of Americans of Middle Eastern descent by their own neighbors. In doing so, cultural critics Arthur and Marilouise Kroker (2001) claim the "low tech," "viral power" of the terrorists was "understandable only in the language of the media: the twin spectacles of sadness and terror; the doubled language of fascination and dread...[and in the media's eventual] shift to the viral language of rage and revenge" (p. 2). Given the magnitude of destruction and the threat to national security, President Bush closed the nation's borders, placed the military on alert, and declared war without consent from Congress. Nevertheless, with the exception of one dissenting vote, both houses of Congress backed his decision, as did 90% of Americans surveyed by pollsters. The mass media had accomplished its task with impunity. With such overwhelming consent, what room was left for dissenting voices?

In homes, classrooms, and workplaces throughout the United States, every aspect of daily life was read through those horrifying images of ecoterrorism. After the attacks, in its moment of commercial savvy disguised as altruism, Hollywood halted the production and distribution of films that were considered questionable due to their gratuitous violent content out of concern that such imagery would further exacerbate the heightened level of fear the terrorists created. Similarly, radio stations pulled songs such as Elton John's classic "Benny and the Jets," The Gap Band's "You Dropped a Bomb on Me," and Dave Matthews Band's "Crash into Me" in deference to the public's sensitivities to violent signifiers. Were such actions and displays based on ethics or commercial opportunism? Has violence in the news, art, and entertainment been naturalized to the point that the mass media is complicit with any form of ecoterrorism? The uncanny resemblance between the terrorists' blasting into the World Trade Center with hijacked jetliners and the visual vocabulary of Hollywood mass destruction films and the mass media in general certainly warrants such a question.

Addressing the power and impunity of images, cultural critic Susan Sontag (1978) argues that the "limit of photographic [mass media] knowledge of the world is that, while it can goad conscience, it can, finally, never be ethical or political knowledge" (pp. 23–24). As such, the perfunctory and biased representations of the mass media either ignore or quickly exonerate any discrete, hidden forms of ecoterrorism in favor of the spectacular images surrounding events such as were experienced on Tuesday, September 11, 2001. As Ross (1994) suggested about the human and environmental devastations of the Gulf War, many images of ecoterrorism remain untold given the desire to preserve a utopian conception of our economic, military, and political supremacy in the world (p. 327). Although cultural critic Dion Dennis (2001, p. 2) declares that our faith in these images of superiority crumbled with the Twin Towers and will continue to do so as the "virus of terrorism" spreads across international borders, we argue that the pervasive nature of these images and their often uncontested position in the mass media continually reaffirms their superiority.

Given that terrorism in all of its manifestations represents "war" perpetrated on the all-encompassing "body," the body human, the body politic, and the body earth, Goat Island's "eco-performance" *The Sea & Poison* challenges our understanding of images and their power to affect our lives and the life of the planet. What this performance and the collective's collaborative work processes suggest is the attainment of what is often deemed impossible: a compassionate, nonviolent, interdependent, and sustainable relationship with the earth. As such, the "impossible tasks" performed in *The Sea & Poison* serve as ecological imperatives, focusing not on the "known but of the unknown; of things impossible; of limits and barriers which cannot be crossed" (Barrow, 1998, p. 1). Paradoxically, the physical and conceptual challenges in Goat Island's work "make possible" a liminal, contingent, and ephemeral space within which social and historical assumptions, commodity fetishism, the stereotypical representations of mass mediated culture and the limits of knowledge can be exposed, examined, and critiqued through performance art.

In *The Sea & Poison*, and in Goat Island's radical teaching practices, the impossible task uncovers these limits of human understanding and enables new perspectives on reality. "The impossible is a powerful and persistent notion," claims science philosopher John D. Barrow (1998, p. 11). The performance of impossibility requires the "courage to create," to leap into the unknown *in spite* of our fears, doubts, and despair, argues psychologist Rollo May (1975, pp. 3, 12). In doing so, it enables the crossing of thresholds from assumed and familiar territories of knowledge to unfamiliar ones where ideas, images, and actions for sustaining a compassionate and caring relationship with the environment can be imagined and created. When describing the importance of impossibility in his *Freeman Etudes* in 1983, composer/musician John Cage stated:

Figure 3.1. Goat Island, *The Sea & Poison*, 2000. Photo by Claude Giger.

These are intentionally as difficult as I can make them, because I think we're now surrounded by very serious problems in society, and we tend to think that the situation is hopeless and that it's just impossible to do something that will make everything turn out properly. So I think that this music, which is almost impossible, gives an instance of the practicality of the impossible. (quoted in Goat Island, 1998, introduction)

We were in the first row as if sitting on the riparian edge of a river or tidewater as Goat Island performers Karen Christopher, Matthew Goulish, Bryan Saner, and Mark Jeffreys entered the compressed space of *The Sea & Poison* dressed in what appeared to be dark factory uniforms. There they commenced their exhausting impossible dances, turbulent nonvirtuoso awkward and erratic movements forcefully twitching, gyrating, leaping, twisting, stretching, and thus exposing their bodies' vulnerability and its limitations. Karen rose from a table, walked over to Matthew, and began leaping, jumping up and down as high as she could go. Matthew followed after her, as did Bryan and Mark. All four configured a quadrangle while jumping in unison. Matthew then danced a variation by rotating his body while bending his knees, followed by Karen, Bryan, and Mark performing the same actions. After each had completed his or her part, they returned to their leaping, jumping up and down in unison, taking turns rotating on the floor, covering their eyes, flailing their arms. Their bodies were hysterical and desperate, yet ironically choreographed in their structured movements.

Matthew, Brian, and Karen suddenly stopped and stood still, while Mark lay on the floor, his body writhing, and his hands persistently slapping the floor. After Mark stood up, all four spread their legs and spun their bodies onto the floor in unison. Karen and Mark immediately leaped to their feet and returned to a jumping routine. Bryan and Matthew joined in. As they continued this routine, their bodies tired and the crescendo of their heavy breathing resonated throughout the space. Matthew and Bryan stayed in place and jumped their bodies while Karen and Mark walked to a corner of the performance space and somersaulted, lay on their bellies, and began wriggling their torsos with their arms lifted. The sounds of their shoes while jumping were like those of marching troops. Punctuated with the sounds of heavy breathing, they suggested "danger" to the body on the one hand, and the "desperation" of the body on the other.

While performing these physically impossible tasks, a complex narrative, a "sea" of disjunctive images and ideas about ecoterrorism began to rage, their conjunctions implying interconnections between nature and culture, the earth and the human body, and their mutual poisoning, degradation, and death. According to performance critic Stephen J. Bottoms (2000), "The world of *The Sea & Poison* is not the shiny, exciting, virtual world of information superhighways, but the dirty, sweaty, poisoned, exhausted physical world of expanding global capitalism" (p. 4). To this oppressive list one can add the egregious acts perpetrated at the World Trade Center, the Pentagon, the downed jetliner in Pennsylvania, and countless others that are likely to occur as the United States and its allied forces wage a protracted war to annihilate future threats of ecoterrorism with ecoterrorism.

The more we lost ourselves in the performance, the more associations of ecoterrorism became apparent. The physical struggle and exhaustion, which we felt viscerally in our own bodies even while sitting in our comfortable seats, suggested complex metaphors about environmental devastation. In doing so, the simple yet impossible tasks of *The Sea & Poison* transformed before our eyes into a performance of ecological imperatives, the body taking desperate measures physically and emotionally, socially and politically, doing the impossible when struggling to survive. Complementing the valiant attempts of the performers' bodies, we interpreted the following narrative about insecticide in the performance as both the poisoning of the body human and the body earth, an exposure of its devastation, as well as its denial:

MARK: Now I want to tell you something. Have you ever been accidentally exposed to any kind of germ spray? In particular, an insecticide, a great deal of insecticide?

KAREN: INSECTICIDE... (*repeats with force as if to underscore the word*)

MARK: Exactly. Has there ever been a time when you were so exposed?

KAREN: Do you remember that day I came home and told you about the truck?

BRYAN: Yes. About two months ago.

KAREN: I was on my way to the store through a back alley. As I was walking a truck turned in. It was spraying trees. Do you think that's what's causing to. . . .

MATTHEW: No, that was only the beginning. You see something happened to that insecticide after it was in your system. Something fantastic and unprecedented. Something which in layman's terms so affected the insecticide that from a mildly virulent germ spray it created a deadly reversal of the growth process. Have you been exposed to any type of radioactivity in the past six months?

KAREN: Oh no, of course not. I don't come in contact with anything like that. I work in advertising.

Only later did we learn that *The Sea & Poison* received its impetus from a particular experience of one of the "Goats," Bryan Saner, who was poisoned by a small creature while hiking with his family in the Grand Canyon. Assuming that culture and nature are ecologically linked as a single body, the pollution of one suggests the pollution of the other. Although Saner's life-threatening experience was unbeknownst to us when we saw the performance, the impossible tasks and narratives in *The Sea & Poison* strongly suggested overcoming, surviving some kind of corporeal adversity.

Goat Island's performances signify through simultaneous linguistic processes. Where one concept is used to represent another, the impossible tasks and narratives serve as metaphors of Saner's desperate attempt to survive poisoning. A second, equally potent form of representation Goat Island used is metonymy, where a concept is used to represent another with which it is contingent and contiguous. Thus, while still a metaphor, the same impossible task functions as metonymy as the goats are physically exhausted, an actual experience, which is contiguous with their performing, their bodies.

The Sea & Poison is a live assemblage of disjunctive images, ideas, and actions whose conjunctions insinuate the poisoning of the body, the environment, and the soul. In the beginning narrative a man with "two heads," suggesting two minds, gives birth to a mutant frog-child. Later, a dancing and talking bear, Bryan Saner with his shirt pulled over his head, alludes to the domestication and exploitation of nature. Raining frogs bring to mind God's "rein of terror" to free Moses and the Israelites from bondage described in Exodus 8:1–15. In another humorous segment of *The Sea & Poison*, while standing in a dark portion of the performance space, Matthew takes a canister filled with earth and pours its contents onto his head. As he balances the resulting mound, he opens a packet of bean seeds, takes one out and plants it into the earth. He then lifts a miniature watering can from the table and sprinkles, irrigating the seed. While holding his head perfectly still, he straps a miniature cassette tape recorder to his waist, extends its small speaker to play soft "elevator" music over the seed. After doing so, he aims a flashlight at the seed to complete the absurd artificial environment for it to germinate and grow. Like a statue, Matthew stands patiently, waiting, waiting, waiting, and waiting for the seed to rise from the earth. After several minutes, and after it appears that his patience has run out, he shouts at the top of his voice.

MATTHEW: There must be some booze in this dump. I'd like a drink. I want a nip. I WANT A NIP. (*Raising his voice even higher, while balancing the wet earth on his head.*)

Bryan's response to Matthew's boisterous demand, "All right Albie. I'll get you one," segues into a narrative about the wounds of waging war. What this transition provides is a double reading of Matthew's actions as being both a heroic ecological act and the feeble attempt of a man gone mad after having experienced the devastating effects of war. In each of these segments, the performance weaves both tragic and comedic elements, and in doing so creates a conflict, a conceptual and emotional crisis in the audience.

This simultaneity of meaning, which is derived from the impossible tasks and narratives, compels a multiplicity of interpretations that challenge "the body's submission to socially prescribed behavioral patterns" (Bottoms, 2000, p. 10). Compared with the mass media's surveillance, objectification, and violent representation of body spectacles, the impossible tasks of Goat Island are performed "in the first person" to expose and critique the residual, reifying effects of mass media representations on the body. In fact, the impossible task may be considered a "dance of resistance." Using their bodies' memories and cultural histories, what cultural critic Susan Sontag (1980, p. 116) refers to as "ruins" when describing the source of Walter Benjamin's writings, the collective performs compelling stories with and through their bodies in the face of the mass media to counter its spectacle (Garoian, 1999, p. 70).

Given that the impossible task is ever present in Goat Island's repertoire as a complex form of representation, it continually reveals new possibilities for meaning, which the collective discovered through its research on toxins. They found that two historical "dances," the Tarantella and Saint Vitus's dance, derived their choreography from the symptoms of poison. The Tarantella was traditionally danced "to rid the body of tarantula poison" and Saint Vitus's dance is the name of an epidemic believed to have originated from "the mass consumption of darnel contaminated bread" during famine years in Italy. "Both of these 'dances' perhaps lasted until the body collapsed; in the first case, purged; in the second, destroyed" (Goat Island, 1998, p. 1).

Goat Island's use of such paradoxes, and conceptual bipolarities exposes and enables an ecology of disparate images, ideas, and actions to interact within the mind, to "beg the question of each other," and in doing so reveal the hidden, unimagined, and impossible. According to Rapoport (1967), the role of paradox is significant in making the impossible possible:

> Whenever, in any discipline, we discover a problem that cannot be solved within the conceptual framework that supposedly should apply, we experience shock. The shock may compel us to discard the old framework and adopt a new one. It is to this process of intellectual molting that we owe the birth of many of the major ideas in mathematics and science [and art]. (p. 50)

Thus, through the physical impossibility of Goat Island's exhaustive tasks and the conceptual impossibility or challenge of interpreting the collective's disjunctive narratives, we "experience shock." This cognitive and physiological condition of the mind and body, which cultural critic Shoshanna Felman (1992) refers to as a "crisis in knowledge," challenges our assumptions and "compels" us to imagine and create ways in which to escape the paradox. Although the derivations of the impossible tasks are unknown to the audience, they nonetheless signify in powerful ways. This was certainly evident in *The Sea & Poison* as Goat Island performed "complex gestures [that] comprised dynamic abstract [and enigmatic] rhythms and patterns of the body and presented the possibility for multiple readings and interpretations" (Garoian, 1999, pp. 88–89).

What underscores the ecological substance of Goat Island's work is a sustainable process of collaboration through which the collective's members engage in dialogue, improvisation, and a critique of significant issues about contemporary culture and environmental politics when developing their performances. As Bottoms (2000) describes it, Goat Island's working process is inherently ecological in that it begins:

> simply with a "seed," a deliberately open-ended question or instruction from director Lin Hixson, each member of the group will offer a response to that seed as being laterally connected to the seed idea. Group members then respond, in turn, to the responses, and so on and so on as the connections expand outwards in a multiplicity of directions. As the material for a performance accumulates, more and more links and cross-references become apparent between the different trajectories.... Having been gradually, intuitively pieced together through an almost organic process of collective development, rather than the dictates of some ruling theme or purpose coming from a single creative mind, Goat Island's performances may be accessed and read in very different ways by different spectators, depending on the mental route one takes in traversing the performative landscape. (p. 5)

Such radically democratic access and interconnections are predicated on an epistemological shift, which anthropologist Gregory Bateson (1972) referred to as an "ecology of mind," a critical form of consciousness that is capable of an empathic stewardship for both human and nonhuman existence on the planet. For Bateson ecology is a process of mind and body whereby ideas and images interact, play, and suggest new possibilities for stewardship and sustainability. By comparison, the loathing of impossibility is ironically made possible by inertia of mind, cognitive states yoked by reified and often fanatical assumptions, which preclude creative and new possibilities for sustainability being imagined and implemented. Insofar as assumptions are bound by familiarity, according to Bateson, they represent an "explanatory world of *substance*[, which] can invoke no differences and no ideas but only forces and impacts" (p. 271). The sedentary desire to resist change and to protect oneself from ideas, images, and actions, which are considered unfamiliar and consequently impossible, is caught in a dichotomy between the familiar and strange, the possible and impossible.

Bateson (1972) argues that contrary to the familiar, possible, and explainable a "world of *form* and communication [exists, which] invokes no things, forces, [or] impacts but only differences and ideas" (p. 271). To characterize this differentiated ecology of mind, he turns to "double bind theory," which "asserts that there is an experiential component in the determination or etiology of schizophrenic symptoms and related behavioral patterns, such as humor, art, poetry, etc.," and which are indistinguishable from one another (p. 272). His metaphor of schizophrenia signifies a "genus of [nonpathological] syndromes," an ecology of mind that he also refers to as "transcontextual":

> It seems that both those whose life is enriched by transcontextual gifts and those who are impoverished by transcontextual confusions are alike in one respect: for them there is always or often a "double take." A falling leaf, the greeting of a friend, or a "primrose by the river's brim" is not "just that and nothing more." Exogenous experience may be framed in the contexts of dream, and internal thought may be projected into the contexts of the external world. And so on. For all this, we seek a partial explanation in learning and experience. (pp. 272–273)

The disjunction of impossible tasks and the fragmented narratives of *The Sea & Poison*, as well as those in other Goat Island performances, creates a "double take" response in the audience, a partial familiarity and explanation, which leads them to their own memories and cultural histories to interpret the performance. The "partial explanation" to which Bateson (1972) refers suggests knowledge that is not fully consummated or realized unless it is considered transcontextually with knowledge that is unfamiliar and impossible. "Thinking out of the box" and "breaking the boundaries," between what is known, familiar, and habitual and that which is not requires "feedback loops...a process of *trial and error* and a mechanism of comparison" (p. 274).

Through trial and error, however, we also learn to rarify, habituate, and rigidify those outcomes and experiences, which are considered successful, acceptable, and within the realm of possibility. Thus, for Bateson, the bifurcated economy of trial and error is "biologically and/or psychically expensive" (p. 274). Error cannot be denied its role in this economic structure insofar as it challenges and resists those outcomes and experiences, which have become rarified, habitual, and rigid:

> The very economy of trial and error which is achieved by habit formation is only possible because habits are comparatively "hard programmed," in the engineers' phrase. The economy consists precisely in not re-examining or rediscovering the premises of habit every time the habit is used. We may say that these premises are partly "unconscious," or—if you please—that a *habit* of not examining them is developed. (p. 274)

For Goat Island, a conscious, reflexive reexamination of habit during the collaborative process enables a breakthrough to occur so that what was previously considered strange and impossible can be imagined, explored, and created within the realm, or context, of possibility. Such breakthroughs are made possible through Goat Island's transcontextuality of mind, an epistemology that considers the interpersonal, collective relationship of ideas, actions, and bodies as liminal, continent, and ephemeral. Such a relationship for Goat Island is immanent in the exchange that occurs as the collective's members interact with each other through a process of intervention, which creates a breach and untangles the double bind of trial and error—that is, escapes its paradox:

The aspect of impossibility in the dances derives from both the oddity of each individual movement, and the complexity of the precisely timed structure of the assembly of the movements into a dance. The actual human performance results in a style of ongoing failure and adjustment during each moment of each impossible dance. (Goat Island, 1998, p. 5)

To maintain such a decentered state of mind and body, the collective tactically disrupts its structure of rehearsal and performance with images, ideas, and actions that create a disparity that requires reflexivity and recapitulation. Unlike the ideology of ecoterrorism, which decenters the mind and body to "divide and conquer," Goat Island's interventions take nothing for granted. They behoove the collective to sustain a collaborative, contingent process that continually re-members, re-considers, re-presents its actions based on the circumstances of the body and its relationship to its cultural and natural environment. Thus, through this reflexive process for determining the impossible dances, Goat Island exposes the tension between trial and error and in doing so disrupts and challenges our assumptions and expectations of what is possible for and with the body.

The interrelational process espoused by Bateson (1972) and Goat Island's collaborative ecology corresponds with artist and writer Suzi Gablik's (1991) imperative for the "reenchantment of art." In challenging the reductive and nihilistic tendencies brought about by the mechanization, economy, nationalism, consumerism, militarism, individualism, and patriarchy of Modernist art, she argues for a paradigm shift in how artists think and engage with the world. Thus, whereas Bateson focuses arguments on a more general "epistemic" premise, Gablik aims for an "aesthetic" shift brought about by community-based and ecologically sustainable processes to bring forth a mythic and spiritual significance in art, its reenchantment.

At the heart of Gablik's proposal is the principle of collaboration—an open, interrelational process of art making. Predicated on empathy for others and stewardship of the planet, this inclusive, compassionate process enables imagining and realizing a sustainable relationship with the environment by searching for a "common ground." According to Gablik (1991), "art moved by empathic attunement, not tied to an art-historical logic but orienting us to the cycles of life, helps us to recognize that we are part of an interconnected web that ultimately we cannot dominate. Such art begins to offer a completely different way of looking at the world" (p. 88).

Similarly, Goat Island's collaborative process opens the discourse and practice of art to mythic and spiritual ideas, images, and actions that exist beyond the boundaries of our socially, historically, and economically constructed assumptions of art, those which we considered impossible, doubtful, and marginal. For Gablik (1991), collaboration is essential in realizing an ecology of mind because it requires that we consider modes of art making that exist outside the parameters of Modernist aesthetic acceptability and possibility:

> In art...we have an aesthetic framework for those who believe the world is composed of discrete objects, and who are fascinated with the individualized self, but we do not have a process-oriented framework for those for whom the world consists of dynamic interactions and interrelational processes. (pp. 162–163)

Her process-oriented framework for art making corresponds with Goat Island's collaborative processes and Bateson's transcontextuality of mind, an ecology of mind and body, which suggests "a continuous flow of mutually determined interactions: the self-in-relationship" (Gablik, 1991, p. 173). Given that we live in a culture that has historically assailed "individualism" to cult status, which considers the Modernist ideology of "independence" and "autonomy" as the sole basis for artistic freedom, Goat Island's interdependent performances of impossibility are reenchanting.

Paradoxically they remind us that impossibilities often serve as thresholds to the possible, that in spite of our individual desires, the quality of our lives and our humanity is enhanced by the cultural differences that we encounter as we interact with and interdepend on others when building communities. Such interaction and interdependency is enabled through a willingness to relinquish the controlling ecological economy of our assumptions and behaviors and to allow differing points of view to "intervene" and enable a more inclusive ecology of mind to exist. This paradox is consistently revealed for audience members and workshop students as Goat Island strategically disrupts its own performances and curriculum with disjunctive interventions the purpose of which is to destabilize logic and rationality and, as a consequence, de-center our persistent individualism, independence, and autonomy. Doing so disrupts the expected, the assumed, and requires an "intelligence immanent in an ecosystem" to interpret and assimilate the disjunctive idea, image, or action the collective introduced (Bowers, 1993, p. 103).

Building on Bateson's and Gablik's ecological imperatives, educator C. A. Bowers (1993) challenges the Western cultural myth of an "anthropocentric universe" wherein human beings are of central importance and the biosphere serves as a resource for achieving their purposes (p. 76). The problem with the current discourse on ecology, he argues, is that its anthropocentric focus contributes to binary, Cartesian assumptions, which set humans apart from the environment and ignores their interdependent, biotic relationship. Bowers claims that even in the most radical of pedagogies, which effectively critique the imperialistic impulses and practices of institutionalized schooling and corporate capitalism, the discourse concerning critical citizenship is centered on human agency with little or no mention about environmental concerns.

Invoking the ecological theories of Aldo Leopold, Bowers (1993) claims that an ethics of cultural work should not preclude an "ethics of land" (p. 139). For Leopold (1970), "land...is not merely soil" but an essential part of a "sustained circuit" in which all living forms are interconnected (p. 253). The epistemological shift that de-centers the human from its current Cartesian moorings and re-contextualizes it within a biotic community is imperative for the survival of the planet. For such a possibility to occur, Bowers suggests looking toward traditional cultures such as those of Native American and aboriginal peoples around the world whose patterns of behavior are radically different than ours. Nevertheless, Bowers heeds a warning about mimicking and trivializing these native cultural practices:

> The process of identifying cultural patterns of more ecologically sensitive cultures...should not be viewed as dictating

the pathway we must follow. The traditions of other cultures are not like products on a supermarket shelf that we can appropriate for our own use. But understanding that ecologically sustainable cultures appear to share certain common characteristics may help us to recognize that some of our most taken-for-granted cultural assumptions may be an anomaly rather than the main pathway of human history. (p. 140)

Challenging "taken-for-granted" anthropocentric metaphors needs to be a priority in schools. Rather than focusing on the external world wherein all objects and events are essentialized and the body remains a spectator, Bowers (1993) calls for an understanding of culture as a "symbolic ecology" in which objects, events, and humans are interconnected. Such an embodied understanding of the world rejects Cartesian dualism and represents for cultural critic Andrew Ross (1994) the possibility for an "ecology of images," a concept that he borrows from Susan Sontag (1977). For Sontag, the ecology of images is necessitated by their "unlimited resource...[that] cannot be exhausted by consumerist waste" (p. 180).

Similarly, Ross (1994) purposefully conflates image "overproduction and overconsumption" by the mass media with corporate exploitation and depletion of natural resources. Both examples, he argues, diminish "our capacity to sustain a healthy balance of life in the social world of our culture. There comes a point...when one image too many destroys the global 'commons'" (p. 332).

Like Bowers's notion of symbolic ecology, Ross's and Sontag's "ecology of images" challenges an imbalance created by an exponential rise in image production by the mass media. Particularly offensive are images "*about* and *for* ecology" comprised of objectified representations of nature commonly found in ecoadvertising, which commodify ecological concerns and practices and result in what Ross (1994) calls a "greenwashing" of environmental problems (p. 337). Correspondingly, in *The Sea & Poison*, Bryan stands at a microphone like a radio broadcaster and recites and sings a Camay soap advertisement from the 1940s and 1950s.

BRYAN: Did you know that just one cake of Camay, can mean a smoother softer skin? Say, did you know that just one cake of Camay, is the way you should begin? You ought to try it now. You better start today. The Camay mild soap diet is the lovely woman's way. For softer and more glamorous complexion: Camay, Camay, Camay.

By performing this song, Brian mocks those insipid representations found in "beauty" advertisements that objectify women's bodies and whitewash their private concerns and desires to perpetuate the patriarchal myth that "beauty is only skin deep." Moreover, within the context of Goat Island's ecoperformance, the lyrics of this song suggest a whitewashing of environmental concerns that include those of the human body.

As Bryan performs this ad about washing the gendered body, Matthew fits Karen's head with a balding makeup cap as she grips a bowl of dead fish, suggesting the effects of chemotherapy on the terminal body and its coming to "grips" with death and dying. The associations are undeniable. The juxtaposition of these two images corresponds with Ross's notion of greenwashing while the body's health is in question. Such a prepackaged and sterile representation of "ecoconsciousness" is rooted in contemporary multicultural and environmental education, institutionalized forms of curriculum and pedagogy that privilege the expertise of teachers and textbooks and often ignore the diverse memories and cultural histories of their students. "When multicultural and [environmental] educators divorce students from direct engagement in their culture's daily productive endeavors for subsistent self-sufficiency...they museumize [or ghettoize] these cultures," claims education philosopher Madhu Suri Prakash (1993, p. 13). In doing so, students' memories and cultural histories are treated as cultural artifacts or reliquaries rather than critical content in contemporary education. What is needed is an "ecological pedagogy" in which the public, academic content learned in school is interconnected with and challenged by the private knowledge students' bring from home and their neighborhoods and communities.

Ross's contrast between images of ecology and ecology of images corresponds with Goat Island's "ecology of performance," an interconnected and sustained way of thinking, saying, and doing in the world that is driven by an ecological consciousness.

By comparison, "performances of ecology" consist of isolated and autonomous actions that are inconsistent with community and environmental concerns, which are driven by fashion, fad, convenience, and other marketplace rationales. Such insidious circumstances require an "ethics of seeing," claims Ross (1994, p. 330), a means by which to challenge and resist "mental pollution," argues Sontag (1978, p. 24). Similar to Bowers and Leopold, Ross and Sontag call for an "ethics of ecology," whereby images are not taken for granted, but considered as part of a sustainable circuit in which cultural productions and natural resources are interconnected and interdependent.

Was not the performance of ecoterrorism perpetrated on the World Trade Center, the Pentagon, and the downed jetliner in Sommerset County, Pennsylvania, dependent on "ecology of mind"? Was it not the work of a highly interconnected network? Are not the terrorists' efforts to thwart and bring down the United States for the past decade examples of sustainability? Does not their ability to overcome such unimaginable and insurmountable acts represent a high level of brilliance and creativity? The creative act is always already explosive in its collision of signifiers. The *avant-garde* force of Modernist art was predicated on the violence of such collisions. Its purpose was to overthrow and topple the regimes of the established, normative assumptions of art and culture. What is the difference between the creative genius of "artistic terrorism," the perceptual and conceptual disruptions of art, which are celebrated on the one hand, and the creativity behind the downing of the Twin Towers on the other? Are both performances not intended to supplant the power establishment because of its oppressive tendencies? Such questions that may reveal the ethical differences between one creative act and another are seldom dealt with in the mass media, yet they continue to gnaw as the "other" voice in our collective consciousness. If the answers to these questions are in the affirmative, how do we compare the aesthetics of ecoterrorism with those of Goat Island and its performance of *The Sea & Poison?* Do we merely refer to the creativity of ecoterrorism as diabolical and the latter as one of civility? Are these two creative outcomes ethically different from one another? If Goat Island's collaborative work is dependent on humility, compassion, and caring, shall

we say that animosity, anger, and hatred drove the collaborative
work of terrorism?

Assuming a position of reflexive humility, perhaps we should
ask about our own complicity in these terrorist attacks. Unlike
Religious Right leaders Pat Robertson and Jerry Falwell who were
quick to blame the United States (especially feminists and homo-
sexuals) by signifying such abhorrent acts as God's wrath for our
"sins," we argue that no one deserves such treatment. Yet, in the
process of demonstrating our national pride by waving and rally-
ing around the flag, we Americans seem easily to overlook the
possibility that we may have contributed to the degradation of
human and nonhuman life in places such as Afghanistan. What
have we denied about our accountability to the circumstances of
the global community? What have we considered as being out of
the question, impossible, and unacceptable when dealing with
other nations? Given their suicidal tactics, terrorists seem to have
nothing to lose, while we as a nation have everything to lose
including democracy itself. Assuming it worthy of defending,
what kind of democracy lacks humility and critical reflection? We
sometimes assume that the cause of democracy is the only acceptable form of governance around the world, and we participate in
nation-building; in doing so, we determine the civil choices, liber-
ties, and identities of other nations. In our fanatical attempt to
defend "democracy," do we, too, possibly become terrorists?
What would democracy look like if it were a liminal, contingent,
and ephemeral practice?

Unquestionably an ethical difference exists between the conceptual, emotional, and physical collisions Goat Island performed
and those of ecoterrorism. Unlike the hypnotic assault of mass
mediated entertainment, the images, ideas, and actions in performances such as *The Sea & Poison* enable critical reflection and
social responsibility. They challenge us to resist reified ideologies
to sustain an open-ended dialogue within our families, neighborhoods, and the global community. In doing so, they provide a
means by which to reclaim our socially and historically determined identities, as well as to heal the wounds of its inscription
on and oppression of our bodies. By comparison, the fanatical
images, ideas, and actions of ecoterrorism are assumed absolute
and beyond reproach. In doing so, they are deployed as lethal

weapons to control and put an end to speech, to destroy the body human, the body politic, and the body earth. The conjunctions of Goat Island's performances are open for interpretation. As we free-associate the disjunctive elements in performances such as *The Sea & Poison,* we participate in a sustainable ecology wherein our differing yet interdependent cultural perspectives enable multiple yet interconnected interpretations. The conjunctions of ecoterrorism represent a totalitarian ideology whose purpose is to destroy bodies, identities, lives, and the environment. Thus, the differences between the impossible tasks of ecoterrorism and those of Goat Island come down to the latter's performance of humility and its desire for and struggle to achieve a peaceful coexist in spite of cultural and environmental differences. Such a desire is predicated on interconnectivity and interdependency, and in doing so, it contains the re-enchanting promise of Goat Island's impossible ecology.

Art Education in the Silent Gaps of Visual Culture

> The advocacy of silence expresses a mythic project of total liberation. What's envisaged is nothing less than the liberation of the artist from him[or her]self, of art from the particular artwork, of art from history, of spirit from matter, of the mind from its perceptual and intellectual limitations...silence keeps things open.
>
> —Susan Sontag, 1969, pp. 17–18, 20

"Collage is the central principle of all art in the twentieth century in all media," claims postmodern author Donald Barthelme (1997, p. 58). Indeed, the disjunctive narrative of collage, its radical juxtaposition of images, ideas, and actions is employed in the genres of cinema, photomontage, assemblage, video art, installation art, and performance art. Given its ability to entice consumption, it is coincidently the prevailing mode of address by the mass mediated systems of television, advertising, the news, the movies, and the Internet.

Collage enables us to experience everyday life in such a way that its disparate and idiosyncratic fragments resist coalescing into a unifying whole, which philosophers Gilles Deleuze and

The original version of this essay "Art Education in the Silent Gap of Pennsylvania's Economy," was an address delivered by Charles Garoian to the Pennsylvania Arts Policy Colloquium held at the University of the Arts, Philadelphia, Pennsylvania, in October 2004. Another version by Garoian, "Art Education in the Silent Gaps of Visual Culture," is in press as of this writing for the *Journal of Visual Arts Research* at the University of Illinois, Urbana-Champaign.

Félix Guattari (1983) refer to as "disjunctive synthesis" (pp. 12–13). Instead of a totalizing body of knowledge, the composition of collage consists of a heterogeneous field of coexisting and contesting images and ideas. Its cognitive dissociation provides the perspectival multiplicity necessary for critical engagement. Dialectical tension occurs within the silent, in-between spaces of collage, as its fragments, its signifying images and ideas interact and oppose one another. Such complexity and contradiction represent the substance of creative cognition and cultural transformation.

Paradoxically, while the indeterminate epistemology of collage narratives such as artist Robert Rauschenberg's *Monogram* resist synergy; they nonetheless enable the apprehension of unstable and shifting images and ideas that deconstruct assumptions that are socially and historically determined. Art historian and critic Donald Kuspit (1983) argues that this paradoxical character of collage "makes uncertainty a method of creation" (p. 129). For science philosopher Michael Polanyi (1983), the knowledge that occurs in such uncertain conditions is "tacit," in that it anticipates the "indeterminate implications... of an approaching discovery" (pp. 24–25). Just as the uncertainty of collage narrative raises compelling questions in creating and interpreting art it can also enable students' critical intervention in the diverse political and economic "collage" of visual culture.

In her installation *and i swore i wouldn't scream...*, The Pennsylvania State University art student Alexandra Sullivan presents a collage narrative wherein the mutability in the in-between spaces of its rarified, "frigid" fragments engages viewers' unassuming conversations and interpretations. The installation consists of a miniature video monitor imbedded in a stack of raw, frozen meat strips at the bottom of a freezer. As viewers peer into the freezer, they see video footage of an egg with its hard shell being pierced and its soft yolk oozing out contrasted against the stiff, frozen meat. The tiny video monitor appears like an eye returning the gaze of viewers' from the "flesh of its body," which in frozen confinement implies incarceration. Violence to the egg suggests the "blinding" and emptying of "vitreous humor" from the omniscient "eye of television." Sullivan's collage narrative evokes questions and suggests multiple interpretations that relate to the abusive practices by the science and meat industries on animals,

Figure 4.1. Alexandra Sullivan, *and i swore i wouldn't scream...*, 2004. Photograph courtesy Alexandra Sullivan.

issues about world hunger, the sexual objectification of women's bodies, and women's abortion rights.

Considering the surfeit of ephemera available in visual culture, virtually every classroom teacher has employed collage as a quick, easy, and inexpensive image-making process. However, the aesthetic dimension of collage is little understood at any depth in schools, and it is within this dimension, in the in-between spaces of collage fragments, that a critical pedagogy is possible.

In the epigraph at the beginning of this essay, cultural critic Susan Sontag (1969) suggests a correspondence between the "open" phenomenon of silence and the empty open spaces of collage. She argues, "'Silence' never ceases to imply its opposite and to depend on its presence ... so one must acknowledge a surrounding environment of sound or language in order to recognize silence" (p. 11). This was certainly the case with composer John Cage's *4′ 33″* during which the performer sat at a piano and played nothing. In other words, the meanings of silence are defined by the cultural context in which it is situated and by never ceasing to imply its meanings are indeterminate (p. 11). To illustrate,

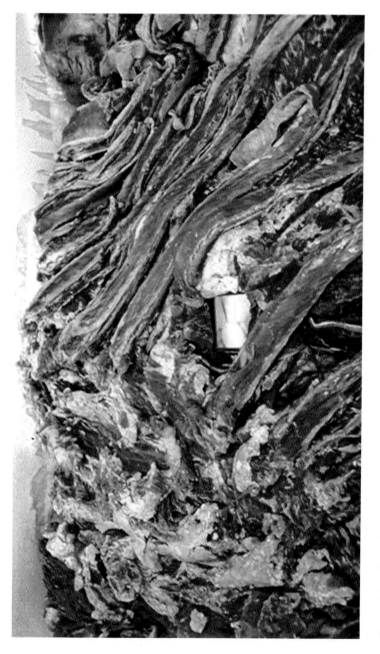

Figure 4.2. Alexandra Sullivan, *and i swore i wouldn't scream . . .* (detail), 2004. Photograph courtesy Alexandra Sullivan.

Sontag points to the "beauty of [comedian] Harpo Marx's muteness [and how it] derives [meaning] from his being surrounded by manic talkers" (p. 11).

Religious historian James P. Carse's (1986) characterization of silence resonates with Sontag's "open phenomenon." Carse refers to the indeterminacy of silence as a form of "infinite play." Compared with "finite play," which imposes rules that bring the speech of others to an end, infinite play "observe[s] rules as a way of continuing discourse with each other" (p. 9). Carse warns that the termination of infinite play results in "unheard silence," which is "not the loss of the [other's] voice, but the loss of listeners for that voice" (p. 32). He writes, "The contradiction of finite speech is that it must end by being heard. The paradox of infinite speech is that it continues only because it is a way of listening. Finite speech ends with a silence of closure. Infinite speech begins with a disclosure of silence" (pp. 110–111).

Like in the muteness of Harpo Marx, the interpretations possible in the empty, in-between spaces of collage narrative remain closed and unheard unless they are disclosed and derived from the manic talking of their surrounding fragmentary images. Critical theorist and filmmaker Trinh T. Minh-ha (1999) refers to these silent interstitial spaces of collage as "the third interval" where the struggle, the dialectical tension between its surrounding fragmentary images, makes possible manifold interpretations (p. 43). In other words, the third interval provides us with room to talk, space within which to respond and challenge the manic talking of the fragments' assumptions and ideologies.

For educator Elizabeth Ellsworth (1997), the dissociation afforded by the disjunctive narrative of collage serves as pedagogical necessity in fostering critical thinking in students. Ellsworth argues that modes of address, like those of collage narrative, resist quick and easy conclusions. The discontinuity of their differing images and ideas impels an "analytic dialogue" as compared with a "communicative dialogue." The "oscillating, slippery and unpredictable" characteristics of analytic dialogue allow for diverse perspectives and unlimited creative possibilities unlike communicative dialogue, which ends in resolution by striving for finite understandings (pp. 115–116).

Because collage has such historical significance in the visual arts, the pedagogical responsibility for teaching about its aesthetic dimension lies in the visual arts classroom where students can learn about its undecidable narrative within the context of art making, art history, art criticism, and aesthetics and further explore and examine their interdisciplinarity across the "collage" of school curricula and visual culture. The importance of collage notwithstanding, left to a "cut-and-paste" mentality, the conceptual profundity of its narrative is easily misunderstood as a pastiche of essentialized images and ideas. Without an understanding of its conceptually compelling process, its criticality, collage ends in nostalgic sentimentality, an immutable notion of history that philosopher Friedrich Nietzsche (1957) argues prevents creativity from occurring (pp. 17–20).

Artist Cristin Millett's investigations into the history of medicine, namely its gendered stereotyping and stigmatizing of women's bodies, is an example of the critical history Nietzsche called for. In Millett's recent installation *Teatro Anatomico*, she created three concentric ellipses whose panels are covered with a skin of sheer chiffon, suggesting the sensuality of the female body as viewers gaze into its interior. Viewers' walking in the labyrinthine space of the installation implies their movement through the passages of the body. On reaching the center of the installation, viewers find a chandelier Millett constructed whose multifaceted forms represent the female reproductive system as they literally and metaphorically "illuminate" the interior space.

Projected on an examination table below the chandelier is a video image of a female body undergoing abdominal hysterectomy. As viewers gaze at the image of the surgical procedure, a surveillance camera captures the image of their faces and streams it live onto the prone body of the patient. In doing so, viewers' awareness of being viewed, exposes their own complicity in objectifying the female body as viewers. As a parody of Renaissance anatomy theaters that objectified the human body and led to the medicalized classifications of health and normality during the Enlightenment, Millett's *Teatro Anatomico* exposes, examines, and critiques historical tropes of the gendered body and in doing so it raises questions about privacy and voyeurism.

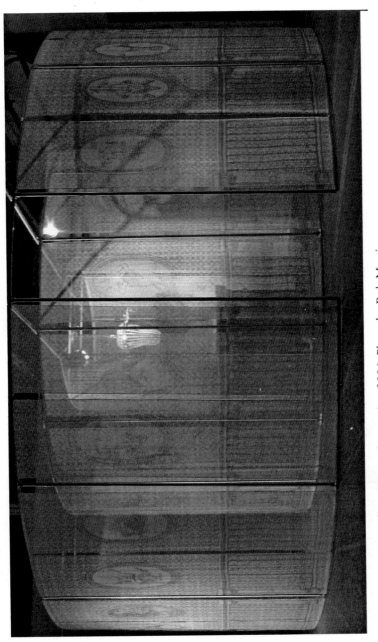

Figure 4.3. Cristin Millett, *Teatro Anatomico*, 2004. Photo by Rob Martin.

Figure 4.4. Cristin Millett, *Teatro Anatomico* (detail), 2004. Photo by Rob Martin.

Important for art educators to consider is Nietzsche's (1957) "critical" conception of history, which in corresponding with the oppositional characteristics of collage narratives such as Millett's installation provides "the strength to break up the past, and apply it, too, in order to live" (p. 21). Bringing history back to life in this way is a haunting prospect. While the fragments of collage provide us with the comfort of fixed signs and familiar codes of cultural history, the undecidability of their in-between, empty, silent spaces conjures *horror vacui*, a fear of empty places, which the philosopher Aristotle characterized as nature's abhorrence of a void and its continual effort to fill it. During the Middle Ages, the Catholic Church invoked *horror vacui* through the work of its manuscript illustrators who filled the empty spaces of their illuminations with canonical images to indoctrinate their congregations and to prevent any free associations that might deflect their faith toward worldly thoughts. The fear of empty places also evokes *tabula rasa,* the Enlightenment concept of education philosopher John Locke put forth in which the mind was presumed an empty slate on which reasoned knowledge was to be inscribed.

Educator Parker J. Palmer (1998) describes such epistemological horror as the "fear of live encounter" (p. 38). Perpetuated in schools, it consists of a "fear of diversity," "fear of conflict," "fear of losing identity," and a "fear of changing our lives" (p. 38). For Palmer, critical thought in the schools is made possible within a paradoxical space where an oppositional tension exists. For that tension to occur, Palmer builds the following six paradoxes into his teaching and learning spaces:

1. The space should be bounded and open.
2. The space should be hospitable and "charged."
3. The space should invite the voice of the individual and the voice of the group.
4. The space should honor the "little" stories of the students and the "big" stories of the disciplines and traditions.
5. The space should support solitude and surround it with the resources of community.
6. The space should welcome both silence and speech. (p. 74)

A critical art pedagogy based on the undecidable narrative of collage offers the kinds of paradoxical spaces that Palmer is suggesting. For that paradox to exist, the discipline-specific content of art should be juxtaposed with the other academic disciplines in schools and the images and ideas of visual culture so that the dialectical tension between them yields multiple critiques, interpretations, understandings, and applications.

Such boundary-breaking education is transdisciplinary because it enables unlikely creative and intellectual associations. It is transpersonal because it recognizes a diversity of learning abilities and allows for students' expressions and performances of subjectivity. It is transcultural because students' memories and cultural histories are recognized as significant content in the classroom and allowed to interplay and intersect with one another as they expose, examine, and critique the commodity fetishism of visual culture and the academic knowledge taught in schools. Hence the critical pedagogy of collage enables students to transgress and transform academic and institutionalized assumptions into new cultural understandings and representations.

Misfit Pedagogy of Visual Culture: A Depraved Obsession with Pictures

> If we want to understand the power of pictures, we need to look at their internal relations of domination and resistance, as well as their external relations with spectators and with the world.
>
> —W. J. T. Mitchell 1994, p. 324

> Stand still—hold it.
> Smile for the camera!
> Say "cheese!"
> FLASH!
> OK, fantastic!

While smiling into a camera with smug expressions on their faces, gloating and gesturing with their thumbs-up, two U.S. military guards assigned to Baghdad's notorious Abu Ghraib prison pose proudly next to a pyramid, an architecture of contorted naked bodies that they have erected using several Iraqi

This essay was first copresented at the Tenth Performance Studies International Conference in Singapore in June 2004 and another version was copresented at the National Art Education Association Conference in Boston, Massachusetts, March 2005. The section at the end of the chapter (pages 80–83) that describes the student performance *Milking Metaphors* is from a previously published article by Charles Garoian, "Performing a Pedagogy of Endurance" (Fall 2002), in the journal *Teacher Education Quarterly*, 29(4), 161–173.

73

prison detainees after concealing their identities by covering their heads with a sandbag.

> Hold it right there!
> Smile—say "cheese" again!
> FLASH!
> Great!

These same guards, again with thumbs-up and smiling, stand behind yet another permutation of the pyramid constructed of naked Iraqi prisoners' bodies stacked atop one another with their buttocks exposed and aimed at the camera. The photographer snaps the shutter. Like big game hunters, a pictorial trophy records their conquest. What is it about taking photographs? What is the obsession about being in pictures?

> Again, are you ready?
> OK, yes.
> Say "cheese!"
> FLASH!
> Got it!

This time, one of the guards with a cigarette dangling from the corner of her mouth, smiles toward the camera, thumbs-up on one hand and with the index finger of her other hand she points at the penis of a detainee whose head is covered with a sandbag and whose naked body is forcibly posed against the prison wall standing abreast with other naked detainees apparently waiting their turn.

> Hold it—hold it.
> FLASH!
> A perfect picture!

A tableau vivant of a detainee's body covered with a dark hood, draped with a black shawl, forced to stand on a small box with wires attached to his hands suggesting torture by electrocution. Indeed, according to some reports, the detainee was warned of being electrocuted if he fell off the box.

FLASH!
FLASH!
FLASH!

In yet another photograph, a detainee has been forced against a cell door. He stands naked in a cowering position as two guard dogs leashed and restrained by military police threaten to attack him. FLASH! A subsequent picture, the next in the series, shows the detainee lying on the floor bleeding after having been attacked and bitten by the dogs. FLASH! Numerous other images picture detainees in humiliating poses forced to masturbate, FLASH, simulate sexual acts with each other, FLASH, or being sexually assaulted by the guards, FLASH, including an image of one detainee who was so distressed by the debased and sadistic actions of the guards that he died. The guards then packed his body in ice and stored it in a shower until the next day when medics arrived and simulated a rescue operation by placing his body on a stretcher, fitted his arm with a fake IV and took him away. FLASH, FLASH. Voluminous pictures, news reports, op-ed columns, photo ops, sound bites, on television, the Internet, in the newspapers, magazines, tabloids, on radio and television talk shows, the spectacle of the mass media delivered a collage of disparate images and texts about the abuses at Abu Ghraib.

Cultural critic Slavoj Žižek (2004) likens the obsession with performing and recording these acts with a "theatricality" that is reminiscent of the spectacle of U.S. popular culture, namely its "obscene underside," the "initiatory rituals of torture and humiliation one has to undergo to be accepted into a closed community" (Electronic version). Although Žižek is pointing to the ritual hazing that commonly occurs on military bases, as well as on high school and college campuses as examples, our collective preoccupation with that "underside" extends to reality TV, the 6 o'clock news, violence and sex in the movies and on television, in other words, our obsession with the spectacle of mass mediated culture. While most of us were focused on the "arrogance" of these guards' egregious acts against Third World people, Žižek pointed out an even more sinister outcome.

In being submitted to the humiliating tortures, the Iraqi prisoners were effectively *initiated into American culture*: They got a taste of the culture's obscene underside that forms the necessary supplement to the public values of personal dignity, democracy and freedom [namely, the higher moral purpose by which the U.S. decided to wage war on Iraq in the first place]. (Electronic version).

Although Žižek found the "initiatory rituals" of U.S. culture culpable in the tortures at Abu Ghraib prison, right-wing radio talk show host Rush Limbaugh dismissed the actions of the guards as a "good time" and an "emotional release." When a caller compared the tortures with a "college fraternity prank," Limbaugh responded with his usual sarcasm:

Exactly. Exactly my point! This is no different than what happens at the Skull and Bones initiation [ironically likening it to President Bush's college fraternity] and we're going to ruin people's lives over it and we're going to hamper our military effort, and then we are going to really hammer them because they had a good time. You know, these people are being fired at every day. I'm talking about people having a good time, these people, you ever heard of emotional release? You [ever] of heard of [the] need to blow some steam off? (quoted in Meyer, 2004, Electronic version)

Given that videos and an entire series of photographs were produced of a broad range of abuses at Abu Ghraib prison, what were these soldiers thinking? Whereas such abuses have been and continue to be commonplace in U.S. prisons and those around the world, what compelled these military guards to construct and document these acts of humiliation in photographs? Why the pictures? Would discretion have mattered? Ironically, "terror" for the United States seems to have become a strategy in its "war on terror." Some news reports alleged that the Pentagon, as an interrogation strategy, condoned these images of prisoner abuse, their sexual degradation and torture in Abu Ghraib to force prisoners to confess their involvement in terrorist activities or to reveal those of others. Were these soldiers merely scapegoats for what the government ordered as these reports suggested or was their obsession, their moral depravity, driven by a personal narcissistic impulse or compulsion for taking and being in pictures? Or, did a larger force within contemporary cultural life drive their obsession?

According to journalist Seymour M. Hersh (2004a), the illegal abuses of detainees by soldiers of the 372nd Military Police Company and by members of U.S. military intelligence were "systematic" (p. 43). A highly secret operation that Secretary of Defense Donald Rumsfeld approved, "encouraged physical coercion and sexual humiliation of Iraqi prisoners in an effort to generate more intelligence about the growing insurgency in Iraq" (Hersh, 2004c, p. 38). If the government sanctioned the depraved acts at Abu Ghraib prison, an equally important question to consider is the military's rationale for deploying the mass media, its spectacle power in the waging of war.

In addition to the military presence at Abu Ghraib prison, U.S. civilian contractors, namely the Titan Corporation and CACI International, were present against whom human rights lawyers have filed racketeering lawsuits because their employees "conspired to execute, rape and torture prisoners during interrogations to boost profits from military payments" (CBS News, 2004 Electronic version). The performance objectives of these contractors corresponds with performance theorist Jon McKenzie's (2001) neologism "perform—or else" that points to the "high performance" expectations of big business, government agencies, and educational institutions and the dispensability of workers if they receive low performance ratings (pp. 5–6).

Why the pictures? Why the Internet? Why the mass media? According to cultural critic Susan Sontag (2004), the "preferred current American way of war-making" through photography and television is "expanding" (pp. 66–67). The "imbedding" of journalists in the wars in Afghanistan and Iraq is confirmation that "war-making and picture-taking are congruent activities" (p. 66). Hersh (2004b) claims that appeared to be the case at Abu Ghraib prison where the photographing of the detainees was "not random but, rather, part of the dehumanizing interrogation process [sanctioned by the Pentagon]" (p. 43).

After the news about the abuses at Abu Ghraib broke out on CBS's *60 Minutes (2)*, CNN, ABC, CBS, NBC, the FOX Network,

CNBC, every news channel broadcast a steady stream of the humiliating images photographed by the U.S. prison guards via television and the Internet. While pundits debated whether these images should have been revealed to the public, Secretary of Defense Rumsfeld announced that the worst were yet to be seen and during a private session of Congress, Senators previewed and decided against making them public.

Cameras are now everywhere in war. They are commonplace among soldiers. According to Sontag (2004), "where once photographing war was the province of photojournalists, now the soldiers themselves are all photographers—recording the war, their fun, their observations of what they find picturesque, their atrocities—and swapping images among themselves and e-mailing them around the globe" (p. 27). The pervasive use of photography by the media and by the terrorists and by the U.S. military prison guards suggests that cameras have become such ubiquitous instruments of surveillance, reconnaissance, and warfare that they are functioning as portable, roving, all-seeing "Panopticons."

In characterizing the "major effect" of philosopher Jeremy Bentham's infamous conception of the Panopticon,[1] critical theorist Michel Foucault (1995) writes that it was intended "to induce in the inmate a state of conscious and permanent visibility that assures the automatic functioning of power" (p. 201). With regard to the abuses at Abu Ghraib prison, the hooding of prisoners' identities certainly parallels Bentham's principle that:

> power should be visible and unverifiable.... Visible: the inmate will constantly have before his eyes the tall outline of the central tower from which he is spied upon. [At Abu Graib the prisoners knew that the photographs were being used to humiliate them.] Unverifiable: the inmate must never know whether he is being looked at any one moment; but he must be sure that he may always be so [having been hooded, the inmates were unaware about what, where and when they were going to be abused]. (p. 201)

The camera as a commonplace instrument of modern warfare suggests a willingness and desire to engage in surveillance as a primary means by which to objectify and claim victory over an enemy—an enemy being "caught in the act" of perpetrating violence, such as the globally televised terrorism of 9/11, or violence being acted out on the enemy, such as that at Abu Ghraib prison. The willingness and desire "to see or to be seen," through surveillance, as mentioned, corresponds with sociologist Mark Juergensmeyer's (2000) "theater of terror" where spectacles of violence serve as *"performance events*, in that they make a symbolic statement, and *performative acts,* insofar as they try to change things" (p. 124):

> [Terroristic acts are] intended to illustrate or refer to something beyond their immediate target: a grander conquest, for instance, or a struggle more awesome than meets the eye . . . to produce a graphic and easily understandable object lesson. Such explosive scenarios are not tactics aimed at an immediate, earthly, or strategic goal, but dramatic events intended to impress for their symbolic significance. (p. 123)

Juergensmeyer's (2000) idea that performative acts of terror "try to change things" corresponds with the aim of disciplinary incarceration, which Foucault (1995) argues "produces [political anatomies, or] subjected and practiced bodies, 'docile' bodies" (p. 138). Certainly the detainees' bodies at Abu Ghraib prison were subjected to a practiced, rehearsed torture, but not limited to disciplinary purposes alone, but to perform for the camera, the portable Panopticon.

The deployment of spectacle as weaponry to enact the recent wars in the Middle East first began with the stunning, globally televised images of al-Qaeda's terrorist attacks of 9/11 and continued with the United States' retaliatory bombings of Afghanistan, then the furious hunt for Osama Bin Laden, then "toppling the Taliban," then the kidnapping and subsequent execution by terrorists of American journalist Daniel Pearl in Karachi, then the futile search for weapons of mass destruction and the subsequent preemptive war on Iraq, then the sudden capture of Saddam Hussein, then the terrorists' horrific train bombing in Madrid, then . . . then . . . then . . . then . . . then . . . and as of this writing, with the abhorrent acts perpetrated by U.S. guards at Abu Ghraib prison in Iraq and the retaliatory televised brutal beheading of independent U.S. businessman Nick Berg, the deployment of spectacle continues.

Everything that is said and done has become a photo op. Spectacle begets spectacle. Neither those so-called U.S. soldiers nor their terrorist counterparts questioned their inhumane actions. They did not stop. They did not question. In not doing so, they clearly intended to create a spectacle of the enemy through a process of demonization or "satanization," the aim of which Juergensmeyer (2000) defines as "reducing the power of one's opponents and discrediting them. By belittling and humiliating them—by making them subhuman—one is asserting one's own superior moral power" (p.183). Given that torture is now broadcast through the spectacle of television and the Internet, the intent is to perform global terrorism.

The Abu Ghraib prison guards kept taking more and more pictures. Geneva Conventions, what Geneva Conventions? Reporting further on the Pentagon's secret program, Hersh (2004c) writes: "The Bush administration had unilaterally declared al-Qaeda and other captured members of international terrorist networks to be illegal combatants, and not eligible for the protection of the Geneva Conventions" (United Nations, Electronic version, p. 41). Apparently the treatment of prisoners of war is no longer determined by internationally agreed on rules, but by those of the spectacle of mass media culture. Clearly the circumvention of the Geneva Conventions led to the brutalization of detainees at Abu Ghraib prison by U.S. military police and military intelligence, which in the end equaled or surpassed the atrocities Saddam Hussein perpetrated against his own people. As Barbara Ehrenreich stated in her 2004 commencement address at Barnard College, "we didn't displace Saddam Hussein; we replaced him. And when you throw in the similar abuses in Afghanistan and Guantánamo, in immigrant detention centers and U.S. prisons, you see that we have created a spreading regime of torture—an empire of pain."

Political scientist Stephen J. Cimbala (2004) places the blame for the actions of these few military guards within U.S. culture. He argues that these actions are symptomatic of "the increased tolerance in American culture for publicly disgusting and obscene behavior; the actions of authority figures toward those whose careers or lives are held in their trusts; and...the example of our own treatment of prisoners in American jails and the conditions of their incarceration" (p. A–6). Regarding his first reason for the guards' depraved actions, Cimbala points to the spectacle of the mass media and our obsessive consumption of its culture:

> What appears routinely today on network television channels, never mind cable, is stupefying. Acts of demonstrative pubic lewdness, crassness and barbarism are spiced with commercials for ever more expensive products, trinkets for the bovine class of consumers with large libidos and no taste...and where sex is light, violence is heavy—we revel in blasted corpses, gouged eyes, broken limbs and sadistic punishments, so long as it's against approved classes of "bad guys."...Add Hollywood to the preceding checklist of symptoms, but multiply by five. The net effect: an evisceration of public standards of propriety. Celebrities in all professions now compete to see who can be the grossest for the mostest. (p. A–6)

There is a disparate yet all-at-once-ness concerning the televised images about which Cimbala writes. They are experienced as segments of a mass mediated narrative consisting of the news, sitcoms, dramas, ads, sporting events, talk shows, and programs about the arts, food, history, wildlife, MTV, and reality TV. The relationships of these narratives are dissociative and uncanny. The segmentation of mass mediated culture constitutes a dynamic, ever-expanding collage of historical and contemporary representations whose interstitial spaces are haunted by the specter of institutional knowledge, commodity fetishism, and government intervention, a condition of corporate capitalism.

Borrowing from the spectral concepts of Karl Marx, critical theorist Jacques Derrida (1994) characterizes the segmented medium of mass mediated culture as a *"spacing* of public spaces," a " dimension of performative interpretation" in which its disjunctive narrative is "irreducible." "Neither living or dead, present or absent: it spectralizes." As such its "hauntological" conditions afford an exorcism of ideology, a critique of its oppressive content and the enabling of creative and political agency as the "interpretation [of its narrative]...transforms the very thing it interprets" (p. 51). According to critical theorist Nchamah Miller (n.d.) "Hauntology and spectrality work deconstructively as radical critique to question critical forms of dichotomies, obstructing totalities, and dialectics, by fragmenting rigid conceptualizations and totalities" (Electronic version).

Numerous Internet authors have referred to the haunting dichotomies, totalities, and dialectics of the Abu Ghraib images as a "collage," including Shakirah Esmail-Hudani (2004), a senior at Harvard University, who writes that the "violence of the camera" [at the prison] was "made all the more disconcerting because of its perverse parody; its pastiche; its collage of reality—pain and humiliation—with its staged antithesis" (Electronic version). Esmail-Hudani's characterization fits most of what constitutes mass mediated spectacle. Where does one enter into a dialogue with the segmentation of visual culture, its collage narrative, to question not only its egregiously depraved content, which both Cimbala and Esmail-Hudani have pointed out, but also the seductive and all-consuming power of its disjunctive visual form?

In his critique of the tortures perpetrated at Abu Ghraib, Iraqi artist Salah Edine Sallat challenged such hauntings by painting a mural in which he ironically juxtaposed the image of the Statue of Liberty, a U.S. icon of freedom and social justice, with the image of the Abu Ghraib detainee who was hooded, cloaked, and attached to electrical wires by U.S. military guards. In place of the "torch of liberty," Sallat painted an electrical switch, a circuit breaker that Liberty flips to send a current of electricity to the body of the wired detainee. In doing so, his painting serves both as a metaphor of the tortures at Abu Ghraib as well as the U.S. military intervention in Iraq.

Like Sallat, the graphic artists of Forkscrew.com are also repulsed by the tortures at Abu Graib prison. Unlike Sallat, in whose mural the hooded detainee is wired to the Statue of Liberty, the poster of the same subject by Forkscrew is wired to Apple's *iPod* ad concept, thus implicating U.S. corporate advertising and consumption in the tortures and the war on Iraq. While the hooded figure in Forkscrew's poster is silhouetted in black against an electrified color like Apple's *iPod* ads, the brand name for the digital music player has been replaced with *iRaq*, and a hand grenade substituting for Apple's corporate logo. At the bottom of the poster the tag line reads, "10,000 Iraqis killed, 773 U.S. soldiers dead" as a signifier for accountability about lost lives.

Figure 5.1. Salah Edine Sallat, Mural, 2004. Photograph by Ramzi Haidar, AFP, Courtesy Getty Images.

The Forkscrew poster of the hooded detainee is one among several mounted in public places as guerrilla actions that parody and protest the social and political injustices in Iraq the U.S. government and corporate advertising perpetrated. In the words of the Forkscrew graphic artists, "It's about refusing to let the sluts in the military-industrial complex and the sluts in the halls of advertising power set the terms of debate for a world full of people whose opinions are more diverse, and more revolutionarily diverse, than any political slogan or cookie-cutter image can express" (Forkscrew, n.d., Electronic version).

Critical interventions such as Forkscrew's and Sallat's are imperative when we consider that in a recent survey conducted in early 2004 by the University of Connecticut of more than 100,000 students, nearly 8,000 teachers, and more than 500 administrators from 545 public and private schools, about whether people should be allowed to express unpopular views, 97% of teachers and 99% of school principles said "yes," whereas only 83% of students agreed. Of the student respondents, 50% said that newspapers should get government approval for stories (CNN.com, 2005, Electronic version). The outcome of this study supports our argument that the public discourses of institutionalized government, corporate advertising, and academic schooling are silencing this critical dialogue.

While Sallat and the Forkscrew graphic artists appropriate the collage aesthetic of mass mediated culture, their mural and posters serve as public pedagogy that raises questions about the oppressive cultural assumptions and ideologies, the hauntings that are found in-between the romanticized image of "liberty" and the horrific image of the tortured hooded figure in Sallat's case, and in-between that same image and the corporate advertising and fetishizing of the *iPod* in the case of the Forkscrew poster. Given the undecidability of the in-between spaces of these provocative collage narratives, the interventions of these artists challenge or "exorcise" the "specter of mass mediated culture" with the "specter of critical citizenship."

We leave you with *Milking Metaphors*, a performance artwork by a Penn State art student whose disjunctive narrative of collage critiques the "corporate terrorism" of the mass media (Garoian, Fall 2002, pp. 170–171). Two indistinguishable bodies

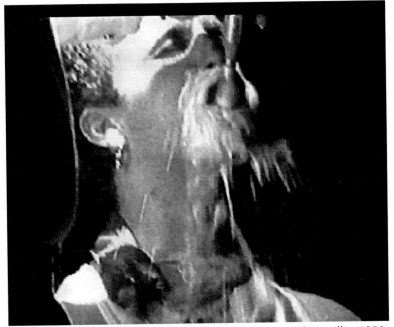

Figure 5.2. James Kesterke, *Milking Metaphors*, (Video still), 1990. Courtesy Charles Garoian.

shuffled across the floor into the center of a sparse, dark performance space. Once they arrived, a light fixture suspended from the ceiling was switched on to reveal an individual with a black hood over his head and dressed in "professional" attire, a white shirt, tie, and dress slacks. Beside this standing figure was James, sitting with his arms, hands, torso, and legs tied to a chair, and his mouth gagged with a strip of cloth. James Kesterke was my student and the hooded person was a friend who had volunteered to assist him in the performance.

All the physical conditions in the space suggested an interrogation room or torture chamber. "Broadcast" from the distant wall behind the two figures was a backdrop of simultaneous sounds, a sonic montage of three tracks. One track consisted of commercial music, sounds, and narratives from television advertisements; a second track was of clips from popular television theme songs; the third track was of miscellaneous clips from various radio stations, representing "the viewpoints of ultraconservative, fanatical, right wing, religious zealots" (Interview with student). As the three soundtracks played in the background, the hooded person suspended a galvanized funnel from the ceiling with a thin rope adjacent to James's head. On the floor next to the chair in which James was sequestered were two 1-gallon bottles of fresh cold milk from the University Creamery across the street.

Like an executioner in a torture chamber, the hooded person untied the gag in James's mouth, pulled his head back and inserted the tip of the funnel into his mouth, opened one of the bottles and began pouring its contents. The duration of the performance from that point on was determined by the time that it took to slowly eliminate the contents of the two gallons. As milk was being forced down his throat, James recited a narrative that was undecipherable, only garbled words and guttural sounds were detectable as he choked, coughed, and spat milk while struggling with his words.

When the three soundtracks had ended and the remaining contents of the second bottle of milk were poured, breathless and exhausted, James reached the ending and only distinguishable phrase of his narrative: "...and justice for all." Only then did the "Pledge of Allegiance," commonly recited in reverence to the American flag, become apparent as the words that James was attempting to articulate. Thereupon, the performance ended with the hooded person turning off the overhead light and dragging James's exhausted body away in the dark while still bound in the chair.

As James claimed during the critique discussion that followed, the point of his performance was "to reference and critique American culture, namely the hypocrisy of the concept 'Land of the Free,' given the hegemonic forces of corporate capitalism, the mass media, and institutionalized religion" (Interview with student). His provocative performance evoked several hermeneutic possibilities. The use of milk as a signifier in conjunction with what appeared as an execution suggested multiple readings: the consumption of mass media and nationalistic propaganda as both nurturing milk and suffocation. It also suggested the drinking of poison and the body's survival using milk as the antidote.

James' professional attire represented the ubiquity of "white collar, corporate America," and the black hood its clandestine, homogeneous façade. James described this type of person as one pursuing the American dream myth, complicit with its nationalistic, corporate, and institutionalized practices as a consumer. Ironically, this complicity was further suggested by the fact that James collaborated with the hooded person in the performance and in doing so insinuated his own hypocrisy.

Although James performed this piece well before the picture-taking incident at Abu Ghraib prison, its uncanny resemblance to the horrific performances at the prison reveals the differences between "disabling" and "enabling" forms of creative and political agency. Given the object of James's performance, *Milking Metaphors*, which was to enable such agency by drawing out and exposing multiple meanings from the visual culture that surrounds him, to critically examine its mass mediated spectacle, and to perform subjectivity through the critical narratives of collage, we ask:

- What is the principle of collage?
- How is it constructed?
- What are its cognitive operations?
- What is the significance of its disjunctive form?
- What is the epistemology of collage and how does it function pedagogically?

Curriculum and Pedagogy as Collage Narrative

Collage is the single most revolutionary formal innovation in artistic representation to occur in our [twentieth] century.

—Gregory L. Ulmer, 1983, p. 84

The function of art isn't to sanction any specific experience, except the state of being open to the multiplicity of experience.

—Susan Sontag, 1969, p. 25

Method of this project: literary montage. I needn't say anything. Merely show. I shall purloin no valuables, appropriate no ingenious formulations. But the rags, the refuse—these I will not inventory but allow, in the only way possible, to come into their own: by making use of them.

—Walter Benjamin, 1999, p. 460

Introduction: Pastiche or Critical Pedagogy?

Although the cut-and-paste technique of collage is pervasive in school classrooms, we have little evidence that any

Charles Garoian has produced three iterations of this essay. It was first published in the Winter 2004 *Journal of Curriculum and Pedagogy*, 1(2), 25–31. Garoian then presented it at the conference Gathering and Trespassing: Interdisciplinary and Critical Investigations of Visual Culture at The Ohio State University Department of Art Education, Columbus, Ohio, November 2004. A later version, "The Critical Pedagogy of Collage," was presented at the Collage as Cultural Practice Conference, University of Iowa, Obermann Center for Advanced Studies, Cedar Rapids, Iowa, in March 2005.

understanding exists of its aesthetic dimensions. Social science teachers assign their students collage to depict the associated events of historical epochs through the cutting and pasting of mechanically reproduced images from magazines, newspapers, and other sources of mass mediated culture. Students' science projects often consist of didactic panels whose compositions are loaded with text, images, and found materials to illustrate the elemental processes found in nature. Health teachers ask their students to create collage representations of the body's physiology and its inner workings to learn about maintaining healthy lives. Mathematics students' use images and texts from magazines and newspapers to visualize quantification and the logic of abstract equations. In each of these pedagogical instances, the understanding sought among the fragmented, disparate remnants of collage is a teleological one that conforms and tames its radical aesthetic to naturalized, academic, and logical outcomes (Sontag, 1966, p.8).

Whereas the pedagogy of collage is widespread in the schools, it is most commonly found in the art classroom. There, students cut and paste away, liberally appropriating images from newspapers, magazines, and other remnants of visual culture often unaware of the conceptual processes in which they are engaged and the lack of critical choices that they are making. Equally disturbing has been the use of collage in art classrooms where students' artistic production is confined to a pastiche, a ready-made aesthetic. Unlike artists who use ready-made cultural materials to critique the hegemony of visual culture, the ready-made narratives found in art classrooms consist of the stereotypical tropes that reinforce the dominant narrative of the mass media.

The pervasiveness of collage in the schools is not a coincidence insofar as the past 150 years of mass mediated culture. Notwithstanding the overwhelming presence of collage in twentieth century art, the creative possibilities it affords is most often trivialized and its epistemological significance left unexamined in art education. Indeed, we will argue that the pastiche pedagogy of collage as defined in the schools contributes to the commodity fetishism of corporate capitalism and the spectacle of mass mediated culture at the expense of subjective critique.

When the pedagogy of collage is limited to serving as a handmaiden to academic culture, as we have described, the understandings of its aesthetic principles are confined to didactic applications and visual entertainments in the classroom. Whereas other academic disciplines may choose to overlook the necessity of collage principles, we find it inexcusable that art educators have basically little or no understanding of the way collage functions as a critical form of pedagogy considering the radical role that it has played in art history since the early twentieth century. Given this lack, the outcome of students' collage works in the schools in general and art classrooms in particular, has consisted of *spectacle mimesis*, stereotypical reproductions that perpetuate rather than critique the spectacle of visual culture.

Our purpose in theorizing collage is to examine its narrative structure as a form of critical pedagogy in art education. Assuming its criticality, collage represents a significant means by which to conceptualize and challenge the seductive yet oppressive regimes of spectacle culture. For philosopher Thomas Brockelman (2001), the undecideablity of collage narrative, its "representational and antirepresentational" character, is "an emblem for contemporary culture" (p. 7). Considering its importance in twentieth century art, why has collage not received the kind of critical pedagogical attention that it deserves in the field of art education? What is the principle of collage? How is it constructed? What are its cognitive operations? What is the significance of its disjunctive form? What is the epistemology of collage and how does it function pedagogically? What impact can an art education based on collage pedagogy have on students' ability to critique the mass mediated spectacle of visual culture?

The artistic invention of collage, followed by photomontage and assemblage, in the early twentieth century, while serving as tropes of the machine age challenged the teleological and synthetic assumptions of art making and disclosed the incongruity of historical and contemporary cultural life. The images and ideas that are radically juxtaposed in these visual art genres constitute a disjunctive *collage narrative* that is "apprehended" rather that "comprehended" through a fugitive epistemological process in which the interconnectivity of its disparate understandings is indeterminate and resistant to synergy. According to art critic and philosopher Donald Kuspit (1983), "concrescence is, in effect, never finished [in collage narrative], however much there maybe the illusion of completion" (p. 127). Creative cognition under the circumstances of collage undergoes a continual state of becoming as the dialectical interplay of conflicting signifiers is experienced and their furtive meanings are apprehended. Hence, "collage...makes uncertainty a method of creation, apparent indeterminacy a procedure," writes Kuspit (p. 129). Bearing in mind its uncertain and indeterminate qualities, in this essay we characterize the narrative of collage as a resource for curriculum and pedagogy.

A complex of visual metaphors, the narrative of collage comprises fragmentary images and ideas appropriated from visual culture whose contradictory meanings are in opposition with each other. As such, collage narrative enables a critical examination of its fragments, namely their contrasting socially and historically constructed assumptions. In the in-between spaces of the fragments of collage, where knowledge is mutable and undecidable, opportunities exist for creative and political intervention and production—a kind of educational research that exposes, examines, and critiques the academic knowledge of institutionalized schooling. Critical educator Elizabeth Ellsworth (1997) conceptualizes these undecidable conditions as unregulated spaces "opened up by imperfect fits between what curricula say we are supposed to be and what we have in actuality not become" (p. 50).

For critical theorist Homi Bhabha (1994), these gaps of intervention represent an indeterminate "Third Space of enunciation," where rarified cultural assumptions are challenged through performances of subjectivity. According to Bhabha, "it is that Third Space, though unrepresentable in itself, which constitutes the discursive conditions of enunciation that ensure that the meaning and symbols of culture have no primordial unity or fixity; that even the same signs can be appropriated, translated, rehistoricized and read anew" (pp. 36–37). Educators D. Jean Clandinin and F. Michaels Connelly (2000) claim that the research of subjectivity in circumstances such as Bhabha's Third Space represents the actions of "narrative inquirers [who] tend to begin with experience as expressed in lived and told stories [autobiographies]" (p. 40).

Bhabha's (1994) notion of the "fixity" of meaning, and the "ambiguity" of interpretation in the Third Space, corresponds with critical theorist Roland Barthes' (1974) concept of "read-

erly" and "writerly" texts. In characterizing the plurality of interpretation, Barthes argues that readerly texts compel cultural consumption and reproduction whereas writerly texts enable the
production of new images and ideas. Barthes asks:

> Why is the writerly our value? Because the goal of literary
> work (of literature as work) is to make the reader no longer
> a consumer, but a producer of text. Our literature is charac-
> terized by the pitiless divorce which the literary institution
> maintains between the producer of the text and its user,
> between its owner and its customer, between its author and
> its reader. This reader is thereby plunged into a kind of idle-
> ness—he is intransitive; he is, in short, *serious*: instead of
> functioning himself, instead of gaining access to the magic
> of the signifier, to the pleasure of writing, he is left with no
> more than the poor freedom either to accept or reject the
> text: reading is nothing more than *a referendum*. Opposite
> the writerly text, then, is its countervalue, its negative, reac-
> tive value: what can be read, but not written: the *readerly*.
> We call any readerly text a classic text. (p. 4)

Hence, according to Barthes (1974), the plurality of meaning that is enabled through the dialectic tension in-between the
disjunctive signifiers of collage corresponds with the writerly
expressions of subjectivity that enable us to re-claim, re-con-
sider, and re-present the rarified representations, the "referendum," of readerly texts according to our personal memories and
cultural histories.

Critical theorist Gregory L. Ulmer (1983) claims that the
indeterminacy of the narrative of collage suggests "silence"—a
space of critique in which codified culture does not predominate
or prevail, but makes possible multiple interpretations and
expressions (p. 102). Similarly, Barthes (1977) regards the plurality of writerly experience as the "death of the author," a silence
that does not presume the end of cultural production, but a plurality of subjective interpretations that challenge an author's
intentions in creating a text. Critical theorist and filmmaker Trinh
T. Minh-ha (1999) describes her experience of silent, in-between
spaces as "jumping into the void, the third interval," which corresponds with Bhabha's Third Space of enunciation. She writes:

I think the only thing that gives me some confidence in what
I do is not what I know ahead of time, but the trust I have
in working with "nothing." This "jump into the void" is a
most exciting moment of enablement, when you know that
everything fragmented and seemingly unrelated around you
can become the film, whose coherence [synergy]—in discontinuity—is due to the fact that "I" constitutes a site where
incongruous things can meet. (p. 69)

Considering its eccentric epistemology, the dialectical tension
of collage narrative provides insight into the interplay between
curriculum and pedagogy—*what* we teach and *how* we teach it.
This curriculum or pedagogy dialectic suggests "curriculum as
collage," "pedagogy as collage," and their "interplay as collage."
Conversely, the narrative of collage may be considered as curricular in its structure and pedagogical in its process. Given such
metaphoric correspondences, the disjunctive narrative of collage
suggests the "impossibility" of curriculum and pedagogy as
opposing binaries.

Literary critic Shoshanna Felman (1987) argues that such
impossibility enables expressions of subjectivity similar to that of
psychoanalysis. She writes, "every true pedagogue is in effect an
anti-pedagogue... because in one way or another every pedagogy
[and curriculum] stems from its confrontation with the impossibility of teaching" (p. 72). Felman's concept of impossibility is not
negative or absolute. Rather, as Ellsworth (1997) suggests, it recognizes "the undecidability of pedagogy [and curriculum], and
the indeterminacy of its address (p. 55). So how does the disjunctive narrative of collage inspire curriculum and pedagogy?

Consider the undecidable meanings and indeterminate
address of video artist Naum June Paik's assemblage *TV Buddha*
(Figure 6.1). A reproduction, a ready-made statue of the Buddha
sits gazing at an image of itself on a television screen, which is
mediated by a closed-circuit video camera. A solipsistic
metaphor, the Buddha stares at the television as the television
stares back at the Buddha as the camera stares at the Buddha.
What does *TV Buddha* signify with its closed-circuit video
system? Could the electronic mediation of visual culture through
television be considered a "closed system" unto itself within

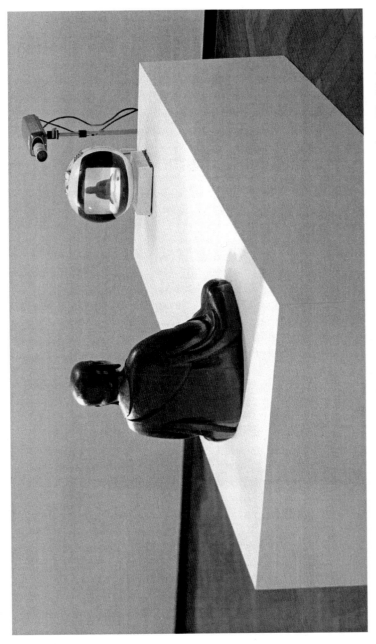

Figure 6.1. Naum June Paik, TV *Buddha*, 1974. Collection of the Stedelijk Museum, Amsterdam, The Netherlands.

which viewers are seduced and anaesthetized by the visual tropes of commodity culture?

What does *TV Buddha* signify with its readymade reproduction of the Buddha within the context of the installation? Is the iconic, canonical state of religion at question? What does the use of a reproduction of a religious icon in the installation signify? What does the juxtaposition of the Buddha reproduction meditating on a television image of itself signify? Is Paik suggesting that religious or philosophical contemplation is as self-indulgent or narcissistic as television viewing? Is television Buddha-like? Is the Buddha experience television-like? Hence the question: to what curricular and pedagogical synergy does the assemblage *TV Buddha* aspire? What is the curriculum of *TV Buddha,* and how do we teach it?

The curriculum of *TV Buddha* is interdependent with its pedagogical address if approached as writerly text. As readerly text, the dialectical tension in-between its obvious signifiers "Buddha," "television," and "short-circuit camera," is imperceptible and incomprehensible. It appears as a pastiche of cultural artifacts. Given this lack of textual interaction, these signifiers remain bonded with their signifieds and their meanings are fixed. As such the Buddha is just a Buddha, the television is just a television, the short-circuit camera is just a short-circuit camera, and Paik's assemblage is just art for art's sake, thereby constituting an intransitive curriculum and a pedagogy the sole purpose of which is the didactic distribution of disconnected fragments of information. When understood according to Barthes' writerly text, the explicit signifiers of *TV Buddha* enable a critical discourse in the classroom whereby a plurality of students' interpretations brings about a plurality of implicit curricular possibilities such as "religion," "transcendentalism," "surveillance," "mass media," "meditation," "narcissism," "technology," "museum," "readymade," and others. Through such intellectual curiosity and reciprocity the narrative inquiry of collage inspires interplay between curriculum and pedagogy.

Furthermore, students' embodiment of this interplay corresponds with Paik having jumped into the void of *TV Buddha*'s collage narrative by having taken the place of the statue in a revised installation of the assemblage at the Projekt '74' exhibition in Cologne, Germany in 1974. Although the concept of embodiment is *metaphorically* understood in Minh-ha's example of jumping into the third interval, at Projekt '74' Paik performed the body *literally*—in explicit ways. In doing so he insinuated his body as one of the conflicting signifiers in the assemblage. Performance theorist Rebecca Schneider (1997) characterizes the space of the "explicit body in representation" as a:

> mass of orifices and appendages, details and tactile surfaces...a site of social markings, physical parts and gestural signatures of gender, race, class, age, sexuality—all of which bear ghosts of historical meaning, markings delineating social hierarchies of privilege and disprivilege. (p. 2)

Thus, by replacing the statue of the Buddha with himself and gazing at his own image through the closed-circuit television system, Paik challenged the concept of the body as the "screen" on which the prevailing codes of culture are continually projected and through which identity is determined. By ostending his body in *TV Buddha,* Paik performed critical reflexivity, a strategy of redress whereby he checked and assumed responsibility for the codes in *TV Buddha*—his own narrative. In doing so, he repositioned the body as a site where creative and political intervention, and production are possible.

Accordingly, the critical reflexivity of Paik's *TV Buddha* performance has important implications for creating a dialectical interplay between curriculum and pedagogy as collage narrative. The indeterminate interplay, between *what* is taught and *how* it is taught, manifests what Ellsworth, Bhabha, and Minh-ha respectively refer to as "in-between" space, a "Third Space of enunciation," and the "third interval," a radically democratic opening where students learn to challenge the academic assumptions of schooling and to create images and ideas based on their differing cultural perspectives, or what Barthes refers to as their "plurality of interpretations." Hence, as students perform their subjectivities in-between the academic disciplines—the collage fragments of schooling—they learn to participate in the democratic process as critical citizens.

The Spectre of Visual Culture and the Hauntology of Collage

... A-A-ART DIED LAST SUMMER.... A-A-ART DIED LAST SUMMER.... WE R-RENTED A COUPLE OF 30—6'S FROM HERB BAUER'S AND WENT H-HUNTING ON THE WEST SIDE.... WE HEARD THERE WAS P-PLENTY OF J-JACKRABBITS, JACKRABBITS RUNNING ALL OVER THE P-PLACE.... WE'D NEVER S-SHOT, SHOT ANYTHING BEFORE.... WE'D NEVER S-SHOT, SHOT ANYTHING BEFORE.... IT WAS A B-BRIGHT SUNNY DAY, IT WAS WELL O-OVER 100 D-DEGREES.... THERE WERE R-RABBIT HOLES THROUGHOUT THE F-FLAT, ARID T-TERRAIN.... THEY D-DISAPPEARED AS WE W-WALKED.... THEY D-DISAPPEARED AS WE W-WALKED.... IN THE D-DISTANCE, ONE S-SUD-DENLY APPEARED F-FROM UNDERGROUND.... AS IF BY INSTINCT, WE R-RAISED AND AIMED OUR R-RIFLES.... WE F-FIRED S-SIMULTANE-OUSLY.... WE F-FIRED S-SIMULTANEOUSLY.... AFTER THE S-SHOTS R-RANG OUT, THERE WAS NO M-MOVEMENT.... WE F-FOUND NO E-EVIDENCE OF A B-BODY.... IT HAD A-ATOMIZED.... IT HAD A-ATOM-IZED.... WE W-WALKED B-BACK TO THE C-CAR, LAID THE R-RIFLES IN THE T-TRUNK.... WE D-DROVE B-BACK TO T-TOWN WITHOUT S-SAYING A W-WORD TO E-EACH OTHER.... A-A-ART D-DIED L-LAST S-SUMMER.... A-A-ART D-DIED L-LAST S-SUMMER.... A-A-ART D-DIED L-LAST S-SUMMER.... A-A-ART D-DIED L-LAST S-SUMMER.... A-A-ART D-DIED L-LAST S-SUMMER.... (See Figure 7.1 on page 101.)

> It is when the language system overstrains itself that it begins to stutter, to murmur, or to mumble; then the entire language reaches the limit that sketches the outside and confronts silence.
>
> —Gilles Deleuze, 1994, p. 28

Originally titled "The Education of the Artist as Public Intellectual," Charles Garoian presented this essay as a keynote address at Big Talk: Community and Conversations in Art and Design Education, Ontario College of Art and Design, Toronto, Canada in April 2005. Garoian and Gaudelius copresented a later version, "The Stuttering Pedagogy of Collage," at the National Art Education Association annual conference, Chicago, Illinois, in March 2006.

A stuttering aesthetic, a pedagogy of disjunctive socially and historically constructed assumptions, is a stuttering not of speech, but of language and knowledge fragments whose gaps offer the possibility for creative and intellectual intervention. It is the "perpetual disequilibrium," the destabilizing force of "creative stuttering" that interests critical theorist Gilles Deleuze (1994), who argues that its rhizomatic structure resists becoming immutable (pp. 24–27). It is the in-between-ness of stuttering, the liminal and contingent conditions of its interstitial spaces, where meaning is always imminent and multiplicity and diversity are possible.[1]

Critical theorist Imma Semetsky (2003) claims that according to Deleuze's metaphor, stuttering creates a "state of a-signifying rupture ... that allows difference to intervene" (Electronic version). Within these ruptures, the other is invoked and "things come to pass and becomings evolve" (Deleuze, 1995, p. 45). This stuttering of language is consistent with the principle of collage in the visual arts whereby decontextualized and recontextualized images, texts, objects, and events are radically juxtaposed, wherein their generative fissures cultural transgression and transformation is possible. The silent gaps in-between the misfit fragments of collage constitute a "not-not" space. They are not-not anything. While appearing an empty abyss, their in-between-ness is imbued with the possibility and hope of creative and political agency.

Based on the premise that the stuttering of collage enables a radical cultural critique, a narrative process that has long been misunderstood and misrepresented in art education, in this essay we revisit its disjunctive aesthetic to argue its pedagogical significance in the education of artists as public intellectuals. In doing so, we use the expressions "principle of collage" and "collage narrative" often interchangeably to represent the larger theoretical context that the critical practices of collage, montage, assemblage, installation, and performance art occupy.

While bearing in mind the creative, political, and intellectual history of collage narrative in the visual arts, we are troubled today about the viability of educating artists at a time when our collective obsession with celebrity, spectacle, and the globaliza-

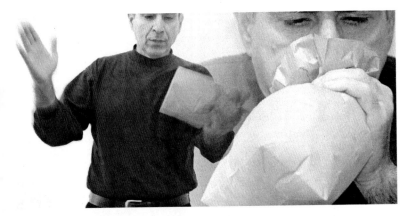

Figure 7.1. Charles Garoian, *hyper/ventilation*, 2005, a live performance about the body's ability to cope with anxiety under the circumstances of information overload about the war. Photo by Rob Martin.

tion of visual culture via the ubiquitous delivery systems of the mass media continues to expand geometrically and dominate the body politic. Cultural theorist Paul Virilio (2000) refers to this take over as the "sonorization" of the body by mass mediated culture; namely the "audio-visual" consumption of the body's attention and its "mutism," a silencing of the body that he associates with cultural imperialism (pp. 69–75). Virilio asks, "How will the silence of the infinite spaces of art subsist" under such conditions (p. 77)? Collage emerges in art when a constant stream of mass mediated images displaces artists' "prolonged attention" (p. 89), erodes their contemplation, and overpowers their critical engagement, which for Virilio represent the attributes of art's silent aesthetic threatened by the silencing aesthetic of audio-visual culture.

The specters of corporate production, advertising, and consumption remain unabated while our students' creative and political agency and their expressions of subjectivity through the practice of art are hindered in the schools. Unquestionably the continual marginalization of the arts through standardized educational reforms and policies such as No Child Left Behind, which was passed in the U.S. Senate by a vote of 87–10 in 2001, is a

clear indication that the unpredictable, indeterminate, and undecidable character of art, its creative and intellectually compelling
force, is unwelcome and must either be conformed to academic,
institutionalized, and governmental understandings of culture or
exorcized from school curricula altogether.

Railing against No Child Left Behind, author Norman Mailer
(2005) maintains that cultural literacy requires the body's mental
and physical attention to reading and writing, seeing and doing,
listening and saying, all of which constitute the understanding
and creation of narrative structures. Mailer identifies the "inter-
ruptions" of commercial advertising on television as the "cul-
prit," which has usurped and altered children's attention and
desire for literacy,[2] thereby, opening the door for the government
to step in and standardize schooling (pp. 4–5). The author cites a
36% increase in television advertising between 1991 and 2003,
which constitutes a hefty dose of 52 minutes of commercials, one
every 7, 10, or 12 minutes, in a 3-hour period (p. 5). He writes:

> Soon enough, children develop a fail-safe. Since the child
> knows that any interesting story will soon be amputated by
> a kaleidoscope of toys, food, dolls, clowns, new colors and
> the clutter of six or seven wholly different products all fol-
> lowing one another in 10-, 20- and 30-second spots, all the
> way to a three-minute break, the child also comes to recog-
> nize that concentration is not one's friend but is treacher-
> ous. (p. 5)

While the standardized testing system of No Child Left
Behind has been positioned to arbitrate educational excellence in
the United States, the issue of cultural inscription, consumerism,
and oppression by the mass media is being ignored in the schools.
Enter a cadre of art education theorists and practitioners who in
recent years have claimed the territory of visual culture as their
domain of pedagogical expertise. Given the predominance and
pervasive influence of the mass media, and the lack of visual and
media literacy and production in the schools, we are inclined to
agree with their proposals about the K–12 art classroom serving
as the disciplinary home where students can learn to expose,
examine, and critique the spectacle of visual culture.

Nevertheless, while these art educators' arguments are well founded, they tend to shift their pedagogical focus from the making of art, as a critical, intellectual practice to those that resemble the interdisciplinary models of cultural studies and media studies. While these models are imperative in the intellectual development of students, before the depth of knowledge and criticality of art practice is subsumed by them, or normalized within the curriculum as a handmaiden to the other disciplines, or thrown out altogether with the bathwater of No Child Left Behind. In this essay we argue that the critique of the spectacle of visual culture is not a new phenomenon in art, but that for more than a century of mass mediation, artists such as the Cubists, Dadaists, Surrealists, Situationists, Fluxus, and others have done so through the critical strategies of collage narrative. Hence, any discussion about educating artists as public intellectuals and critical citizens within the circumstances of mass mediation falls short if the collage theories and practices of these artists are not acknowledged and considered for their critical pedagogical possibilities.

Art historian and critic Rudolf Kuenzli (2005), the curator of the 2005 exhibit, "Interventionist Collage: From Dada to the Present," at the University of Iowa Museum of Art, writes about the major role that the principle of collage has played in "twentieth century art, literature, film, and music from Cubism to Hip Hop" (Exhibition wall text). Kuenzli's conception of the critical role of collage over the past century reveals its creative and political dimensions and the cultural work of its artists as public intellectuals. He writes:

Newspapers were the ubiquitous mouthpiece[s] of ideological representations through the century, but for artists armed with scissors and paste, the ideologies they embodied and disseminated could be literally cut up, rearranged, and thus transformed. Similarly magazines, magnetic tape, vinyl albums, and film footage could be subjected to hands-on manipulations. Through these transgressive and critical manipulations of mass media, the collagist turns from being a consumer of mass media into a creative producer. Collage has proven to be a potentially powerful strategy for intervening in media representation of reality, since it uses socially coded representations and returns them in the form of a new critical contextualization. (Exhibition wall text)

The "critical contextualization" of collage to which Kuenzli refers corresponds with the concepts of "deterritorialization" and "reterritorialization" that critical theorists Gilles Deleuze and Félix Guattari (1987) attribute to the multivalent principle of assemblage (p. 8). According to Deleuze and Guattari, the "multiplicities [of assemblage] are defined by the outside: by the abstract line, the line of flight or deterritorialization according to which they change in nature and connect with other multiplicities" (p. 9). What Kuenzli and Deleuze and Guattari are describing are the workings of creative cognition, which is evoked through the intellectual processes of collage and assemblage. The "outside" to which Deleuze and Guattari refer is the space of otherness, a liminal and contingent space where the socially and historically constructed assumptions of collage fragments are not only "carried away...but also undergo all kinds of reterritorializations" based on the imaginings of personal memory and cultural history (pp. 88–89).

Pennsylvania artist Stacy Levy and her collaborators landscape architect Julie Bargmann, hydrogeologist Robert Deason, and historian T. Allan Comp's ecological artwork, a water treatment park in Vintondale, Pennsylvania, *Acid Mine Drainage & Art, Project for Vintondale* (1995–2003) is an example of how the reterritorializations of collage cognition can transform our understanding about an ecologically devastated landscape in literal and metaphorical ways.

Levy and her collaborators literally changed the pH of the acid mine drainage created by rainwater coming in contact with abandoned coalmines in Vintondale and created an ecological artwork that metaphorically represented the history and the natural beauty that surrounds the site (Levy, Electronic version). Levy explains:

The water treatment park changes the pH of the discharge and allows the heavy metals to dissipate in a series of pas-

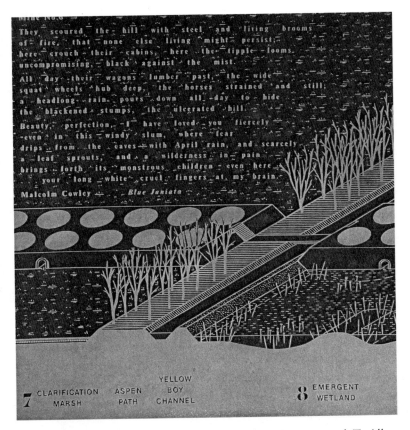

Figure 7.2. Stacy Levy, Julie Bargmann, Robert Deason, and T. Allan Comp, Project plan detail, *Acid Mine Drainage & Art, Project for Vintondale, 1995–2003*. Photo courtesy Stacy Levy.

sive treatment ponds. This design tells the story of the treatment and history of coal mining on the site. In the Litmus Garden, the colors of the fall foliage and bands of wildflowers reflect the changing condition of the water. The huge scale of the mining operation is recalled with raised footprints of each mine building, planted in red twigged shrubs throughout the wetland areas. (Levy, Electronic version)

The process of collaboration among these artists and scholars and their use of site-specific materials and conditions represent the

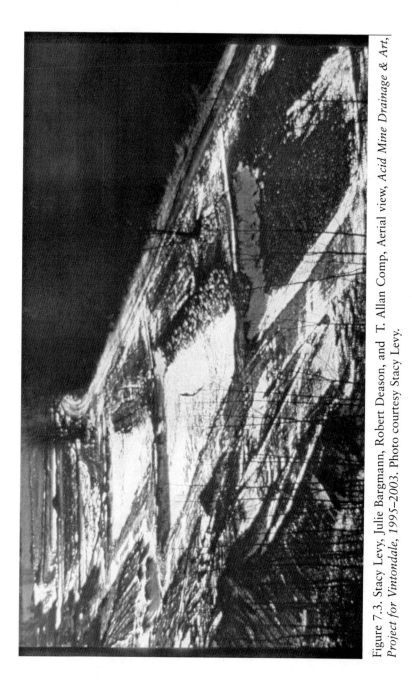

Figure 7.3. Stacy Levy, Julie Bargmann, Robert Deason, and T. Allan Comp, Aerial view, *Acid Mine Drainage & Art, Project for Vintondale, 1995–2003.* Photo courtesy Stacy Levy.

disjunctive characteristics of collage narrative, which in dialectical tension with one another, a "testing of the waters," brought forth creative and intellectual solutions.

Works of art, such as Levy's and her collaborators', in exposing, examining, and critiquing significant issues in contemporary cultural life represent the practice of critical citizenship. "Artists stand at the edge of society," claims cultural critic Carol Becker (2002, p. 18). In her conception of the artist as public intellectual, Becker argues that what we might expect from artists is work that "will impact society, to challenge existing forms, to raise significant questions, to bring ideas into society that might not yet be visible, and to do so in a way that can be accessed, and to some degree understood" (p. 19). Similarly, cultural critic Edward Said (2001, Electronic version) writes that the public role of artists and intellectuals "is to uncover and elucidate the contest, to challenge and defeat both an imposed silence and normalized quiet of unseen power" (p. 4). Becker's and Said's concept of public intellectuality is diametrically opposed to the "mass intellectuality," which cultural theorist Maurizio Lazzarato (1996) claims is "created out of a combination of the demands of capitalist production and the forms of 'self-valorization' that the struggle against [manual and intellectual] work has produced" (p. 133).

Lazzarato (1996) differentiates between the production of commodities via "direct labor" exemplified by Taylorist and Fordist practices, and what today constitutes "immaterial labor," which he characterizes in two ways. First, "informational content of the commodity...refers directly to the changes taking place in workers' labor processes in big companies in the industrial and tertiary sectors, where the skills...[of direct labor are being replaced by] skills involving cybernetics and computer controls" (p. 132). Lazzarato's second aspect of immaterial labor, the "cultural content of the commodity," consists of activities that "are not normally recognized as 'work'...[such as] defining and fixing cultural and artistic standards, fashions, tastes, consumer norms, and, more strategically, public opinion" (p. 132).

Consistent with Lazzarato's conception of mass intellectuality as immaterial labor, cultural critic Walter Benjamin (1968), in the 1920s and 1930s, warned about the threat to public intellectual life by the decline in value of the art of storytelling and the growth of mass communications and its fixation on processing information. Benjamin writes, "[Storytelling] does not aim to convey the pure essence of the thing, like information or a report. It sinks the thing into the life of the storyteller, in order to bring it out of him again" (p. 91). The subjectivity of storytelling to which Benjamin refers parallels the complex and diverse content of personal memory and cultural history, the embodied knowledge brought to bear in the in-between spaces of collage narrative. Writing about the complexity of storytelling he describes a "piling on top of the other of thin, transparent layers which constitutes the most appropriate picture of the way in which the perfect narrative is revealed through the layers of a variety of retellings" (p. 93). Such telling and retelling represented for Benjamin intellectual work that he associated with "teachers and sages" (p. 108).

What is interesting for this discussion are the similarities between educating mass intellectuality as Lazzarato defines it and the "politicized" mass educational ideology of No Child Left Behind, and how they both contrast with Becker's and Benjamin's "political" concept of educating public intellectuals. Critical educator Henry Giroux (1997) distinguishes "politicized" and "political" education as follows:

> Political education means teaching students to take risks, challenge those in power, honor critical traditions, and be reflexive about how authority is used in the classroom. A politicizing education refuses to address its own political agenda and creates silences through an appeal to a specious methodology, objectivity, or a notion of balance. Politicizing education perpetuates pedagogical terrorism; a political education improves the pedagogical conditions for students to understand how power works on them, through them, and for them in the service of constructing and expanding their roles as critical citizens. (p. 265)

A tautology, the politicization of mass intellectuality corresponds with mass mediation, corresponds with mass production, which corresponds with mass consumption. The all-consuming hyperbolic spectacle of the mass media continues to grab a firm foothold in national and international politics. Consider the spectacle surrounding the horrific terrorist attacks on the World Trade Center; then the Pentagon; then the downing of the jet airliner in Sommerset County, Pennsylvania; then the hunt for Osama Bin Laden; the U.S. invasion of Afghanistan; the search and failure to find weapons of mass destruction; then the U.S. invasion of Iraq; the capture of Saddam Hussein; then the gubernatorial election of muscle man/movie star Arnold Schwarzenegger in California; then the tortures, depravity, and obsession with picture taking at Abu Ghraib prison; the funeral of Ronald Reagan; then Martha Stewart's trial for insider trading; Martha's imprisonment, and subsequent house arrest; Martha's annoyance over her ankle bracelet; and then, as if all of that weren't enough....

...Enron's corruption and bankruptcy; the scandalous ads of the Bush and Kerry presidential campaigns; Janet Jackson's "wardrobe malfunction"; the Summer Olympic Games in Athens; the Miss America and Miss Universe pageants; the Academy, Emmy, and Grammy awards; Food TV, MTV, Sports TV, ABC, CBS, NBC, CNN, MSNBC, the FOX Network; steroid use in baseball; the tragic tsunami disasters in Southeast Asia; March Madness; and as of this writing, the child molestation case against Michael Jackson; the embroiled legal and moralistic debates over the life and death of Terri Schiavo; the death and funeral of Pope John Paul II; and the coronation of Pope Benedict XVI; and, and, and, then, then, then...numerous other excesses of mass mediation continue to overwhelm our attention, lure our consumption, intoxicate our sensibilities, and anesthetize our criticality as citizens.

Religious studies scholar Tom Beaudoin (2005) attributes the spectacle surrounding the embroiled legal and moralistic debates about Terri Schiavo's living and dying to an "American cult of celebrity." He argues that by sensationalizing her case the Religious Right exploited Schiavo to create a political platform from which to further its moralistic agenda. Beaudoin claims, "celebratizing morality is one of the ways the powerful manage the governed; it's especially effective because those who are being led appear to take some pleasure from joining in public outpourings of emotion" (p. A10). By virtue of its visceral appeal, the spectacle of celebrity creates a culture of narcissism where one relinquishes creative and political agency to live vicariously and obsessively through someone or something that has been hyperaesthetized.

The consumerist collage of the mass media deconstructs and reconstructs information into disparate, disjunctive sound bites, which are easily assimilated for their entertainment value. In a recent Nike ad, for example, a visually compelling montage of a cobra and a mongoose positioning themselves, bounding from side to side, backward and forward, raise and lower their heads to strike and overcome one another, while in a soft yet sinister voice a narrator warns, "you lose, you die." A thick black line drawn across the floor demarcates the animals' separate domains and in doing so, the ad serves as a classic binary, an either-or, reductive representation of its subject, the object of which is to sell Nike's new Air Zoom Huarache.

Throughout this 30-second, multimillion-dollar advertisement viewers are drawn in by the stunning theatricality of the montage. While its mise en scène constitutes a conundrum about the purpose of the ad, and before viewers have an opportunity to imagine and freely associate with what they are seeing, the fight scene is quickly disrupted with a concluding image. In an attempt to leave no fragment of the montage unqualified, the Nike swoosh appears to ensure viewers' understanding that the corporate logo is the absolute coalescing and coherent signifier of the ad (Deleuze & Guattari, 1987, p. 8). For viewers in the know about March Madness, the swoosh is a clear reminder about Nike's "you lose, you die" corner on the basketball market and virtually every other major sport.

Nevertheless, while the swoosh represents the ad's mode of address for Nike, its colonization of signifiers is less than absolute because the in-between spaces of collage narrative are always volatile (Ellsworth, 1997, p. 38). While the swoosh attempts to manipulate and exploit the reading of the montage for its "profit and entertainment value," it nonetheless exists as one among the several signifying fragments in the disjunctive narrative. The volatility of the disjunctions in the ad thus decentralizes the swoosh's power of address and makes Nike's corporate ethics and practices vulnerable to critical interrogation.

Art critic Donald Kuspit (1983) argues that the indeterminacy of collage, its compositional narrative, does not cohere. As such, "concrescence is, in effect, never finished, however much there may be the illusion of completeness.... The incongruous effect of...collage is based directly on its incompleteness, on the sense of perpetual becoming that animates it" (pp. 127–128). Narrative theorist Martin McQuillan's (2000) characterization of contrapuntal reading and contrapuntal writing corresponds with Kuspit's "incompleteness" of collage narrative. McQuillan writes:

> ...the privileging of one narrative-mark [a collage fragment] over another is not possible because every narrative-mark is only defined by its differential relations to all other marks.... [Hence,] a totalisation of experience by a narrative-mark is impossible, and this impossibility is disguised in the process of editing and selection which creates the imaginary figure of closure. (p. 23)

For McQuillan the differential relations between narrative-marks are predicated on the dialectical tension between narrative and counternarrative. Given that such tension resists closure, its ruptures are where Kuspit's notion of "perpetual becoming" other is animated.

Artist and high school teacher David Young's electronic assemblage *Frequency and Flow* (2004) corresponds with the dialectical tension created in-between the misfit narrative-marks, the fragments of collage, and their resistance to closure. Young's description of his piece serves as a metaphor of creative cognition and the embodiment of intellectual play. He writes:

> The piece consists of an active microphone amplifier projecting the sound of the spark that continuously rises up the gap in the torso of the copper figure within the glass globe. The arc is created using a simple neon sign transformer that creates high voltage yet low amperage electricity that has the ability to be conducted through the air. Such "Jacob's Ladder" devices, seen in science fiction movies, use the heat created by the arc of electricity to increase the conductivity of the air thus allowing it to travel upwards across a greater distance or gap. *Frequency and Flow* represents my aesthetic fascination with antiquated science equipment and sound equipment, and how their previous functions corresponded

Figure 7.4. David Young, *Frequency and Flow,* 2004. Photo courtesy David Young.

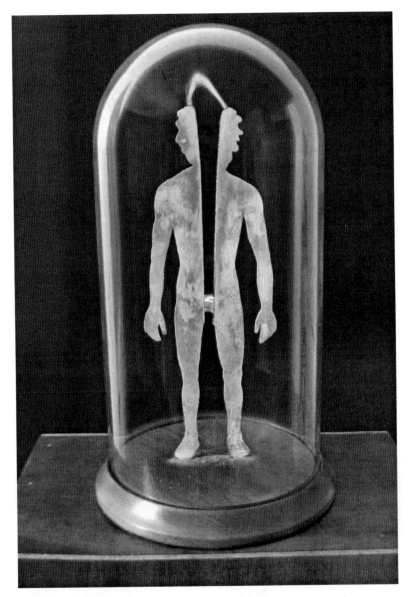

Figure 7.5. David Young, *Frequency and Flow* (detail), 2004, Photo courtesy David Young.

with the energy flow within the human body [and the flow of ideas across memory and history]. One influence is the yogic practice of *kundalini* rising where the energy from the lower *chakras* is moved upwards through the body and beyond the head. Another more general association is the energetic or emotional balance between conflicting parts of the body, the yin and yang, good and bad, or simply this or that, and the way these separations give rise to new states of mental, physical, emotional, and oftentimes spiritual resolution and change. (2005, correspondence with artist)

By suggesting the dialectically charged spark of collage narrative, Young's conception of "frequency and flux" alludes to the "perpetual disequilibrium," and the hope for "things coming to pass" and "becomings evolving," which comprise Deleuze's metaphor of stuttering and Deleuze and Guattari's lines of flight.

Such indeterminacy and the immanent possibilities of collage narrative suggest the "haunting" of its interstitial spaces by specters, ghosts, and apparitions of personal memory and cultural history and the imaginings of creative cognition. McQuillan (2000) contends, "all material excluded in the process of narrative editing and selection installs itself hauntologically within the material which the narrative presents... [and that] the differential relation between narrative-marks [collage fragments] calls for 'discernment' [a conjuring] on the part of the reading subject" (p. 25). Here McQuillan is invoking philosopher Jacques Derrida's (1994) metaphor of spectrality in which Derrida introduces the concept of "hauntology" a pun on "ontology," thus suggesting the interdependence of being and not being, which in turn relates to philosopher Friedrich Nietzsche's (1957) concept of critical history claiming, "man must have the strength to break up the past, and apply it... [in contemporary cultural life] in order to live" (pp. 20–21).

For Derrida (1994) hauntology is an evocative process that enables us to transgress and transform our social and historical moorings. Re-visiting, re-membering, re-conceptualizing, and re-presenting knowledge from the past constitutes a critical conjuring process whereby someone or something invisible, "beyond being," is imagined and imbued with the immanent possibility of becoming other than what we already know. Such imaginings according to Derrida are projected on an "imaginary screen where there is nothing to see.... Not even the screen sometimes" (pp. 100–101), which relates to the evocative character of the silent interstitial spaces of collage narrative.

Derrida attributes the displacement of contemporary political and intellectual life to the specter of mass mediated culture. He argues, the "medium of the media... assures and determines the *spacing* of public space, the very possibility of the *res publica* [the common good] and the phenomenality of the political.... This element itself is neither living or dead, present or absent: it spectralizes. [Whereas] it does not belong to ontology,... [it does require] hauntology" (pp. 50–51). For Derrida, the re-thinking and re-presentation of memory and cultural history via the imaginings of hauntology has moral and intellectual purpose. He writes:

> If he loves justice at least, the "scholar" of the future, the "intellectual" of tomorrow should learn it from the ghost. He should learn to live by learning not how to make conversation with the ghost but how to talk with him, with her, how to let them speak or how to give them back speech, even if it is in oneself, in the other, in the other in oneself: they are always there, specters, even if they do not exist, even if they are not longer, even if they are not yet" (p. 176).

The justice of hauntology about which Derrida writes corresponds with French artist Christian Boltanski's site-specific intervention, *The Missing House* (1990), on Grosshamburger Strasse in central Berlin. Boltanski's piece consists of a break, a hollow cavity in-between an apartment complex where it was bombed in 1945. Having researched the site with his students, Boltanski discovered that the previous residents of the destroyed apartment were Jews. In memoriam, the artist painted the residents' names, dates of birth, occupations, and the date of their death on the remaining adjacent walls of the ghost apartment approximately in the spaces they once occupied. Edward Said (2001, Electronic version) refers to the counterpoint of public intellectual work, such as Boltanski's, as "countermemory, [a] putting forth its own counterdiscourse that will not allow conscience to look away or fall

Figure 7.6. Christian Boltanski, *The Missing House* (detail), 1990. Photo by Charles Garoian.

asleep" (p. 7). In asking viewers to consider those who are absent, Boltanski's intervention honors the memory of the residents while simultaneously evoking, "not forgetting," the horrific specter of the Third Reich.[3]

While compelling examples of collage narrative, such as Boltanski's, are pervasive in the history of modern and postmodern art, its radical aesthetic is trivialized in the schools as a cheap and easy, cut-and-paste method of producing posters, journals, and other instructional ephemera to illustrate and teach academic knowledge in the social sciences, science, health science, mathematics, and other subject areas. Having assimilated television, the Internet, video games, and advertising, students easily fill the gaps in-between the fragments of these discipline-specific collages with the normalized and coherent assumptions abundantly supplied by academic and mass mediated culture. Students have little or no room for culturally diverse memories and histories, the disparate content that they have acquired from their respective families, neighborhoods, schools, and communities to enter in and challenge the silencing epistemology of academic collage.

Cultural critic John Fiske (1992) argues that such distancing of art and intellectual practice from daily life "produces ahistorical meanings of art works and allows the members of its social formation the pleasures of allying themselves with a set of human values that in the extreme versions of aesthetic theory, are argued to be universal values which transcend their historical conditions" (p. 154). By detaching and distancing art from students' personal lives, their memories and histories, and filling them instead with ahistorical and universal assumptions, "academic collage" misunderstands and misrepresents the critical pedagogy of collage, or what critical educators Henry Giroux and Roger Simon (1989) refer to as a "pedagogy of possibility."

> This is a pedagogy that refuses detachment, one that understands how multiple forms of power and experience structure and position different groups in sets of relations that must always be questioned as part of a larger project of extending and improving human capabilities; for a pedagogy that recognizes that teaching and learning represent different aspects of how meaning is produced through the construction of forms of power, experiences, identities that also have wider political and cultural significance. (p. 220)

Subservient to the academic disciplines, the critical possibilities of collage have been silenced in the schools. A zip zoom, pastiche mentality and a cheap expediency have contributed to an indolent pseudo-intellectualism reminiscent of the audio-visual sensibilities Virilio alluded to, rather than the kind of rigor that its conceptual complexity deserves. Such scrapbook mentality is not exempt from K–12 art classrooms where prosaic assignments reduce the radical aesthetic of collage to the mere cutting of newspapers, magazines, and other found ephemera to produce images that seek literal, clichéd, and stereotypical outcomes, which either ignore or overlook its liminal and contingent characteristics; hand turkeys at Thanksgiving and toilet paper Kachina dolls are examples. This kind of cultural relativism ascribed to collage narrative in the schools smacks of intellectual opportunism, an "I can do it, you can do it, anyone and everyone can do it" mentality that presumes a populist conception of art practice, which trivializes the critical dimensionality of art and serves as a referendum to diminish and marginalize its creative, intellectual, and pedagogical significance within the curriculum.

Instead, we argue for a revisiting of the principle of collage in the schools to expose and examine its radical aesthetic as a form of critical art pedagogy by which to challenge mass mediated and mass intellectualized culture. For that to occur, curriculum and pedagogy in art education must first be theorized and practiced as collage, a disjunctive, stuttering process where art teachers' personal and academic understandings are dialectically charged by the multicentric memories and cultural histories of their students. We advocate for a pedagogy of possibility, not one that is modeled after the way our former teachers taught us, but a vigilant creative and intellectual practice such as that of the artist in the studio whose work is paradoxically infused with a healthy dose of skepticism, indeterminacy, and undecidability to continually push the boundaries of existing knowledge and challenge cultural absolutes. Such openness of intellectual curiosity and engagement precludes an insular critique that is exclusive to the culture of art and opens to the "outside" through "multiple lines of flight," which enable students to understand the correspondences between art and cultural work outside of art and their personal lives. It is within the open yet charged spaces of a critical pedagogy of collage that such an education of the artist, as public intellectual, is possible.

The Dis-eased Pedagogy of Disaster Tourism

People are sexually aroused by pictures and sculptures; they break pictures and sculptures; they mutilate them, kiss them, cry before them, and go on journeys to them; they are calmed by them, stirred by them, and incited to revolt. They give thanks by means of them, expect to be elevated by them, and are moved to the highest levels of empathy and fear. They have always responded in these ways; they still do.

—David Freedberg, 1989, p. 1

Virtuality and virality get mixed up in my mind.[1]

—Jean Baudrillard, quoted in Bardini, 2006, Electronic version

On December 26, 2004, the tectonic plates beneath the Indian Ocean shifted triggering a massive earthquake at an extremely rare magnitude of 9.0 on the Richter scale thus generating a cataclysmic tsunami that devastated much of Southeast Asia, killing and injuring an estimated 216,000 people in 14 countries including Sri Lanka, Thailand, Indonesia, the Maldives, and India. CNN, ABC, CBS, BBC, NBC, FOX, MSNBC—all the major and minor networks—reported the horrifying news about the cataclysmic event—minute by minute, hour by hour, day by day.... The deluge was so vast and overwhelming that news reporters and camerapersons were unable to take it all in; aerial views could not contain the sweep of its

---

Charles Garoian first presented a shorter version of this essay at the Twelfth Performance Studies International Conference, Queen Mary University of London, England, in June 2006.

destruction. As with other catastrophic events such as 9/11, the scopic regime of the mass media had once again found a definitive signifier and reinvented itself through the disaster capitalism of "tsunami broadcasting."

Over the course of the following year, 2005, the iconic impact of the tsunami became the scale by which to measure newsworthiness for all the networks. In particular, and beginning with the tsunami, CNN reassigned Anderson Cooper, the commentator of the network's popular news program, *Anderson Cooper 360°*, to travel and report on the spot from any and every corner of the world where disasters occurred by virtue of his youthful, charming, yet seemingly sympathetic and courageous demeanor, thus suggesting a public allure that the network wants to cast about itself.

During the year, in addition to the tsunami, Cooper covered the death and funeral of Pope John Paul II in Rome, the politicization of Terri Schiavo's life and death in Florida, the devastation of Hurricane Katrina in the Gulf states and the earthquake in northern Pakistan, prognostications about a global bird flu pandemic, and the 12 trapped miners who died of asphyxiation in a West Virginia coal mine. Furthermore, from his newsroom on *360°*, Cooper raised the bar on every news event to the level of a global catastrophe—from shark attacks on the Atlantic Coast, to bed bug infestations in New York hotels, to the war in Iraq and Afghanistan, to Natalee Holloway's disappearance in Aruba, and numerous other natural, social, political, economic, and religious "disasters" in 2005.

We too are there on the spot. We embody the site/sight Cooper is experiencing, reporting from, albeit virtually. We go wherever he goes via television and the Internet. We see what he sees and what he shows us. We are disaster tourists and he is our tour guide, our benevolent disaster docent informing us about how to see and understand the excruciating pain of others, which we readily witness on the screen. We dread and are befuddled by the scenes of tragedy at which the camera is aimed and that he ponders with furled brow. The sympathetic murmur of his voice enables us to feel what he feels. His apparent compassion absolves us of any complicity, obligation, or responsibility in the disaster. As we watch, we are hypersensitized by others' misfortunes while being reassured of our own safety, comfort, and privilege of our lives.

As CNN/US President Jon Klein described Cooper to the Associated Press, "[he's] got a refreshing way of being the anti-anchor.... He's just being himself, he's asking the questions you would like answered. He's getting involved the way you might" (de Moraes, 2005, Electronic version). Indeed, our collective involvement in tragic spectacles via the mass media finds its most obsessive and depraved example in the dystopian vision of disaster tourism where tsunami survivors, in exercising entrepreneurship, photographed and sold images of dead bodies found floating in the water or twisted in the rubble (Radical Left.net, 2005, Electronic version). Moreover, foreign tourists flocked to the region to view firsthand and photograph the devastation, and to have their pictures taken along side bloated, mutilated, and decaying corpses as mementos and souvenirs.

In yet another example of disaster tourism, Grey Line New Orleans offered a 3-hour bus tour, *Hurricane Katrina—America's Worst Catastrophe*, of the city's "most misery-stricken spots, including the Superdome, the Convention Center, and neighborhoods ravaged by [the cataclysmic storm]" (Associated Press, 2005, Electronic version). While the voyeuristic tourism facilitated by the mass mediated systems of television, the Internet, and mainstream cinema pales by comparison with these exploitive acts, it is nonetheless complicit in whetting and feeding our insatiable appetite for and complicity in spectacle culture.

Assuming the scopic regime of spectacle culture is a teaching engine that drives visualization, what are its pedagogical objectives? What is the dialectical relationship between its hyperbolic content and its institutional structure? How does spectacle culture inscribe and compel the body's desire and agency? What fuels the signifying power of spectacle, and how does it manifest itself as disaster tourism? If the driving force of spectacle's cultural capital is predicated on the desire for global capitalism, what countermeasures exist to expose, examine, and critique its hegemony and enable creative and political agency? In the remainder of this essay we address these and other questions about the spectacle pedagogy of disaster tourism.

Sociologists John Lennon and Malcolm Foley (2000) refer to the public's attraction to and fascination with death, disaster, and atrocity as "dark tourism." Although they point to historical pilgrimages to religious and secular sites as the earliest forms of dark tourism, in the twentieth century it manifests as a public obsession (p. 8). They attribute the rise of dark tourism with the technological force of modernity and the psychic dislocations of postmodernism's replications and simulations, both of which are implicated in the mass mediation of spectacle culture (pp. 6–8). Lennon and Foley characterize dark tourism in three ways:

> First, that global communication technologies play a major part in creating the initial interest. . . . Second, that the objects of dark tourism themselves appear to introduce anxiety and doubt about the product of modernity [the failure of its science and technology]. . . . Third, the educative elements of sites are accompanied by elements of commodification and a commercial ethic which . . . accepts that visitation . . . is an opportunity to develop a tourism product. (p. 11)

Hence for Lennon and Foley (2000) the mass produced and mediated anxiety, doubt, and commodification of dark tourism constitutes pedagogical objectives that reveal "a fundamental difficulty of delineating education and entertainment/spectacle and an uncritical approach to history" because decisions about educational quality, critique, and credibility remain the purview of "project directors, managers and curators as central to their 'missions' [in commodifying productions]" (p. 90).

Why do we want to go where the spectacle of disaster tourism takes us? Performance studies scholar Barbara Kirshenblatt-Gimblett (1998) points to our desire for escape as an important reason. "Getting away is different from going somewhere. Because escapes are defined as departures rather than arrivals, the actual destination is somewhat arbitrary. The very term 'getaway' or 'escape' suggests that the push away from home is stronger than the pull toward a particular place" (p. 153). Ostensibly, the impulse of disaster tourism is driven by our desire to escape and transgress cultural experiences that are contemptibly familiar to us for those that are catastrophically foreign, exotic, and taboo.

Unfortunately, such transgressions are imperialistic; the gaze of commodity fetishism, the intent of which is the consumption and control of cultural difference, drives them.

Considering that vision and visuality are socially and historically constructed, Anderson Cooper's altered ways of seeing, understanding, and representing global calamity conveyed through the ideological refractions of mass mediation manufactures and shifts our ways of seeing and understanding calamity. Indeed, when calamities are elevated to the level of sublime spectacle as they are by the mass media, distinguishing the facts from the commodification and fetishism of the facts is difficult because of the "aesthetic pleasure that is derived from a depiction of catastrophe, which would otherwise be horrifying to experience in reality" (Mirzoeff, 1995, pp. 60–61).

The sublime ideology of spectacle culture is irreducible, because, according to cultural critic Guy Debord (1995), it "increases according to its own logic...with no end to its growth" (p. 30). As such, the exaggeration and distortion of information as spectacle represents the media's totalizing form of global capital (p. 22). Accordingly, not only are ordinary occurrences hyperbolized through mass spectacle, but spectacle also serves as pedagogical model for how life is to be experienced and understood. Hence, we are always already consumed by the teaching machinations of spectacle culture.

The trope "disaster tourism," as used in this essay appears in three ways. Its first guise is that of telecommuting via television, the Internet, and other mass mediated information delivery systems to the scene of a disaster. This form of tourism is virtual not actual. The body is present at the site of a disaster by virtue of its absence. We are there, but not there similar to how most of us experienced, by virtue of our absence, the terrorists' downing of the World Trade Center vicariously through the media in 2001.

Second, disaster tourism is our normalized obsession with visual culture in which the form and content of its hyperbole functions at a level of grand spectacle. We are always already consumed and constructed by it. Cultural theorist Mikhail Bakhtin's (1984) concept of carnival corresponds with the normalization of spectacle. "Carnival is not a spectacle seen by the people; they live in it, and everyone participates because its very idea embraces all

the people. While carnival lasts, there is no other life outside it"
(p. 7). Similarly, the carnival of disaster tourism values extreme
cultural experiences such as those witnessed through extreme television, extreme cinema, extreme foods, extreme sports, extreme
news, extreme science, extreme makeovers.... Such collective
obsession with spectacle culture is manufactured according to the
political economy of the mass media claim cultural critics Edward
S. Herman and Noam Chomsky (1988):

> The U.S. media do not function in the manner of the propa-
> ganda system of a totalitarian state. Rather, they permit—
> indeed, encourage—spirited debate, criticism, and dissent, as
> long as these remain faithfully within the system of presup-
> positions and principles that constitute an elite consensus, a
> system so powerful as to be internalized [by the general pop-
> ulation] largely without awareness. (p. 302)

Hence, Herman and Chomsky (1988) argue that both the
medium and the message of mass mediation function at such
hyperbolized levels that they manufacture an insatiable appetite
for and obsession with spectacle culture. Later we will discuss
how this obsessive tendency corresponds with critical theorist
Jean Baudrillard's (2002a) concept of a viral condition in which
the body politic is always already infected.

The third guise of disaster tourism occurs with actual travel
to the scene of a catastrophe not for providing aid, but to see and
experience it *in situ*, to claim that one was physically present in
the midst of it all. Is such an act of transgression the fulfillment of
morbid curiosity or the desire for personal transformation, the
rebirth of one's normalized life? In cases where the human body
has been ravaged by accidental or natural calamity, perhaps the
latter is the disaster tourist's motivation for wanting to witness its
grotesque corporeality. Bakhtin (1984) writes about the transgressive yet transformative power of the grotesque body:

> [It] is not separated from the rest of the world. It is not a
> closed, completed unit; it is unfinished, outgrows itself,
> transgresses its own limits. The stress is laid on those parts
> of the body that are open to the outside world, that is, the
> parts through which the body itself goes out to meet the

world. This means that the emphasis is on the apertures or the convexities, or on various ramifications and offshoots: the open mouth, the genital organs, the breasts, the phallus, the potbelly, the nose. (p. 26)

The transformation enabled by the transgression of disaster tourism's grotesque is the premeditation of spectacle production and consumption. What Bakhtin (1984) suggests about carnival and the grotesque body has been co-opted by the mass media to recreate and transform itself in the interest of corporate capitalism. In such instances, the interest of the media is the production and reproduction of the citizenry into critical consumers or discriminating shoppers whose desires and choices are not self-determined, but determined by the ideological regime of media spectacle.

Art historian David Freedberg's (1989) characterization of the stirring power of visual images in this essay's epigraph certainly rings true when we consider the global response to network news coverage of catastrophic events, which consists of a magnitude of stirring that Baudrillard (2002b) refers to as "extreme phenomena" (pp. 67–69). While visual images have always, and will always, stir people emotionally and conceptually, what concerns Freedberg are "those responses that are subject to repression because they are too embarrassing, too blatant, too rude, and too uncultured [too different]; because they make us aware of our kinship with the unlettered, the coarse, the primitive, the undeveloped; and because they have psychological roots that we prefer not to acknowledge" (p. 1). The repression of subjectivity as Freedberg describes it is predicated on the normalization of media culture and its objectification of viewers.

Not only are people stirred by visual images delivered by the mass mediated systems of television, the Internet, cinema, and even video games, but we have also assimilated the narcissism and false consciousness of its extreme phenomena to force our own social, political, and economic agendas on others as witnessed by the tragic events of 9/11 perpetrated by al-Qaeda, the U.S. retaliation in Afghanistan and the subsequent war on Iraq, and as of this writing the angered and retaliatory response of Islam to the Danish cartoon criticizing the prophet Mohammed as a terrorist.

Possessed by media spectacle, we repress and relinquish our subjectivity and criticality to that of its extreme message. "The spectacle of terrorism forces the terrorism of spectacle," declares Baudrillard (2002a, p. 30). Ubiquitous yet insidious, the tautology of terrorism and spectacle ravages the private and the public body's imagination and health.

This totalizing economy of spectacle culture politicizes education in the form of "pedagogical terrorism," claims radical educator Henry Giroux (1996) because it is "determined by a doctrinaire political agenda that refuses to examine its own values, beliefs, and ideological construction" (pp. 126–127). In contrast with "political education," which decenters hegemonic pedagogies, the politicizing force of spectacle culture "marginalize[s] some groups, repress[es] particular types of knowledge and suppress[es] critical dialogue." Such force is threatened by the democratic preconditions of political education, which demands "critical inquiry, risk-taking, and the responsibility to resist and say no in the face of dominant forms of power" (p. 126).

The media is now understood as the most efficient pedagogical forum in which to politicize, instigate, and wage ideological battles, and to attain global dominance by way of its atavistic culture of terror, fear, anxiety, and paranoia, which it effectively manufactures. Although the production and dissemination of visual culture continues to grow exponentially and to dominate our sensibilities, visual and media literacy and criticism is lacking in our schools. This neglect in the schools constitutes a corporate and institutionalized response similar to Freedberg's (1989) concept of repression insofar as it censors and controls knowledge to promote the consumption of visual culture at the expense of critical pedagogy that could enable students' understandings and responses to the power of its images. The repression of students' creative, intellectual, and political agency in this way obfuscates their critical citizenship in a cultural democracy thus perpetuating the commodity fetishism of the spectacle of visual culture and resulting in an acquiescent and paranoid citizenry unable to distinguish between its virtual and viral character.

Baudrillard (2002b) purposely conflates the "virtuality" of information systems and the virality of the body suggesting, ironically, that both are dis-eased:[2]

Virulence takes hold of a body, a network or other system when that system rejects all its negative components and resolves itself into a combinatorial system of simple elements. It is because a circuit or a network has thus become a *virtual* being, a non-body, that viruses can run riot within it; hence too the much greater vulnerability of "immaterial" machines as compared with traditional mechanical devices. Virtual and viral go hand in hand. It is because the body itself has become a non-body, a virtual machine, that viruses are taking it over. (p. 63)

Like Baudrillard, critical theorists Gilles Deleuze and Félix Guattari (1987) also conceptualize the body as a virtual system, a "body without organs," where viral "organisms" accumulate "to impose upon it forms, functions, bonds, dominant and hierarchized organizations, organized transcendences" (p. 159.) So, for Baudrillard and Deleuze and Guattari, the virtual conditions of network systems such as the mass media are rife with virulence as are the bodies to which they are interconnected. With all its idiosyncratic elements eliminated or homogenized to conform to a singular ideological system, the virtual environments of mass mediation functions as a vacuum that lacks internal resistance to ward off the virulent forces of spectacle culture and terrorism. Debord's (1995) characterization of spectacle culture's contagious claim of the body corresponds with Baudrillard's metaphor of the virtual and viral. Debord writes:

The spectacle corresponds to the historical moment at which the commodity completes its colonization of social life. It is not just that the relationship to commodities is now plain to see—commodities are now *all* that there is to see; the world we see is the world of commodity" (p. 29).

Hence, the virulence of Debord's commodity world, which is "*all* that there is to see," corresponds with the virtual world of Baudrillard's "immaterial machine." Both constitute the "colonization of social life."

Considering the virulence of media spectacle and its affliction of the body, issues and concerns about the body's mental and physical health are usually assumed the purview of therapy in art education. Within an art therapy context, the body in all of its manifestations becomes the locus of critique and the artwork an instrument of observation and detection. In such instances, the pedagogical object of art therapy is clinical and diagnostic given that it uses works of art to objectify the body by focusing solely on its pathology and in doing so classifying it as "normal" or "abnormal." Binary tropes such as these delimit the infirmed body's agency insofar as they contribute to its oppression and consequent dis-ease. While the catharsis and exercise of art performance can potentially heal the body of its psychological and physiological infirmities, the condition of its ill health is nonetheless exacerbated as the scopic regime of art therapy objectifies, classifies, stigmatizes, marginalizes, and disenfranchises it as dysfunctional other.

The medicalization of society has politicized the body argues cultural historian Ivan Illich (1976). He claims, "the medical diagnosis of substantive disease entities that supposedly take shape in the individual's body is a surreptitious and amoral way of blaming the victim" (p. 169). Similarly philosopher Michel Foucault (1994) characterizes the medical gaze as profiling and conflating the body with disease. "The patient is the rediscovered portrait of the disease; he is the disease itself, with shadow and relief, modulations, nuances, depth; and when describing the disease the doctor must strive to restore this living density" (p. 15). Considering the scopic regime of the medical gaze, our argument is against pathologizing pedagogies such as art therapy that merely objectify and represent the body as the "disaster tourism" site/sight of medical science in favor of art performance that enables the infirmed body's critical and creative expressions of subjectivity through art for both healing and attaining political agency within contemporary cultural life.

As cultural critic Susan Sontag (1978) suggests, "to rectify" the punitive conceptions of disease, is to "de-mythicize it" (p. 7). Corporeal metaphors that conflate the body with art and science as in *Body Worlds* (2005–2006), an exhibition of actual "plastinated," flayed and displayed bodies by Gunther von Hagens, and the sixteenth-century anatomical illustrations of Andreas Vesalius, dissect, mythologize, and expose the body to ultimate visibility, virtuality, and virulence as Baudrillard, Illich, and Foucault suggest thus making it vulnerable to its conflation with illness and disease. The "cancerous body," "the tubercular body," "the AIDS body," and the "schizophrenic body" are tropes that constitute a wounding through spectacle.

Literary critic Mark Seltzer (1997) characterizes the "mass attraction to atrocity" of disaster tourism as "wound culture," a trauma that mass mediated spectacle afflicts on the public sphere. According to Seltzer the trauma of wound culture is symptomatic of "the public fascination with torn and opened bodies and torn and opened persons, a collective gathering around shock, trauma, and the wound" (p. 3). Such infatuation with grotesque bodies, Bakhtin also suggested, enables spectacle to transgress and transform its own hyperbole to intensify consumption. Seltzer writes that a critical examination of mass spectacle exposes "a traumatic *yielding* to representation (a yielding of bodies and persons to representation intensified to the point of reproduction)...[which] amounts to the 'assault' or 'bombardment' of the subject by the burgeoning materialities of communication, reproduction, and representation" (p. 12). In a vivid example of traumatic yielding to the representational power of wound culture, Seltzer describes the popular television series *ER*

> [as] the world, half meat and half machinery, in a perpetual state of emergency *ER* is an endless series of torn and opened bodies and an endless series of emotionally torn and exposed bio-technicians. There are the endless hook-ups of bodies and appliances; trauma and techno-speak; cardiac arrest and broken hearts. These are the spectacles of persons, bodies, and technologies that make up a wound culture and the scenes that make up the pathological public sphere. (p. 26)

This brief characterization of *ER* is a sample of how Seltzer exposes, examines, and critiques a "traumatic yielding" to the spectacle of wound culture. Like the Apostle Thomas, depicted in Michelangelo Merisi da Caravaggio's *Incredulity of Saint Thomas* (1601–1602), who inserts his index finger into the aberrant wound of Christ's body to question and confirm the spectrality of its return from the dead, Seltzer probes, deconstructs, and reconstructs the pathological narrative of wound culture from his own subject position. While this back-and-forth "switching" from the public sphere of spectacle to his private sphere of subjectivity enables Seltzer to experience, on the spot, the "(worldly) reference, psychosis or sociology" of wound culture, it also enables him to resist its virulent power by virtue of his own "(self-) representation" and self determination (p. 15). Such critical examination constitutes a dis-eased pedagogy of resistance, a counterspectacle that challenges the virulent power of mass culture.

Seltzer's switching between the public and private spheres corresponds with N. Katherine Hayles's (1999) notion of cybernetic signification. Hayles argues that the body's interface with the informatics[3] of mass spectacle constructs it as data thus functioning as a "flickering signifier." In doing so, the flickering body is constituted as "pattern and randomness...[because its] signifier is opened to a rich internal play of difference" (p. 31). This indeterminate and undecidable character of the body's flickering signification represents a dis-eased pedagogy of resistance in countering the fear and loathing of the body as information, which Hayles claims is possible "by attending to the material interfaces and technologies that make disembodiment such a powerful illusion" (p. 47). She goes on to characterize such flickering performance of subjectivity as a "double vision that looks simultaneously at the power of simulation and at the materialities that produce it...[to] better understand the implications of articulating posthuman constructions together with embodied actualities" (p. 47).

This switching between the public and private spheres that Seltzer writes about and the double vision of Hayles's flickering signifiers is characteristic of the ontological shift, the to and fro that takes place between subject and object during the process of play and art making, according to critical theorist Hans-Georg Gadamer (1989). Play is predicated on the movement between one's socially and historically constructed assumptions, one's rationality, and the forces of uncertainty, indeterminacy, and undecidability (pp. 103–104). Gadamer (1986) argues that this to and fro displays a "phenomenon of excess," the presence of absences that constitutes the object of play and art (p. 12). For example, this excess of undecidability is immanent interstitially in collage narrative by way of shuttling in-between its disparate fragments where possibilities of absent meanings and interpretations are not not there.

The phenomenon of excess revealed through dialogic "switching," "flickering," "double vision," "to and fro," and "shuttling" is consistent with the visual distortions of *anamorphism* insofar as these vacillations constitute a dis-eased, critical pedagogy that blurs, smears, and streaks the ideological assumptions of spectacle culture, ironically suggesting a specular rupturing of the sublime terror of wound culture. Because the power of such terror is unstable according to philosopher Edmund Burke (1998), "it may be possible to strip a considerable degree of strength of its ability to hurt. When you do this, you spoil it of every thing sublime, and it immediately becomes contemptible" (p. 60). Critical theorist Slavoj Žižek's (1989) conceptualization of "anamorphic shift" corresponds with Burke's notion of destabilizing sublime terror. Žižek writes, "the 'sublime object of ideology' is the *spectral object*[4] which has no positive ontological consistency, but merely fills in the gap of a certain constitutive impossibility" (p. 76).

Considering that perspectival space constructs and accommodates the gaze within its geometric structure, anamorphism is its inversion, its abstraction, its parody—a spoiling of its specular object as Burke and Žižek suggest, which exposes, examines, and critiques the assumptions of a visually coherent world. Given the scopic refractions of mass mediation, its stretch of influence and construction of the social body, the discomfiting visuality of anamorphism serves as a potent antidote against the virulent, "ideological anamorphosis" of spectacle culture (Žižek, 1989, pp. 99–100). About this critical visuality, Žižek (1997) writes, "the procedure which enables us to discern the structural inconsistency of an ideological edifice is that of the anamorphic reading" (p. 75).

Aberrant stain and *protracted stain*, two examples of structural inconsistency in anamorphism, function pedagogically by enabling critical readings of spectacle ideology. In doing so, the "grotesque" of their specular inconsistencies challenge the grotesque wound of disaster tourism. For example, a dis-eased anamorphic pedagogy is evident in a picture plane when its perspectival space is problematized by a constituent distortion, an aberrant stain as in the sixteenth-century painting *The Ambassadors* (1553) by Hans Holbein. When the gaze of the viewer is perpendicular to the planar surface of the picture, Holbein's representation of the ambassadors standing among the attributes of their enterprise is clearly evident. The anamorphic stain at the bottom of the painting, which deflects and begs the question of the representational image of the ambassadors, consists of a perspectival distortion; a stretching that when viewed from an oblique angle to the plane of the picture is corrected into an accurate representation of a skull. Ironically, the oblique view of that angle conversely distorts the coherence and verisimilitude of the ambassadors' image.

According to artist and theorist Daniel L. Collins (1992), "the act of viewing anamorphic images reasserts that the construction of vision is a dynamic, reflexive, and self-critical operation" (p. 74). Collins characterizes the observer of anamorphic images as "eccentric" and viewing as performative "subjectivity":

> To observe anamorphic images, one must be an "eccentric observer," that is, an observer who is not only a bit "eccentric" in the usual sense of the term (i.e., strange), but an observer who is willing to sacrifice a centric vantage point for the possibility of catching a glimpse of the uncanny from a position off-axis....An eccentric observer is exactly the observer of the anamorphosis, an observer who literally stands apart and is self-aware of the process of seeing. The vantage point of the eccentric observer is not a refutation of a centric viewing position—it is its shadow. It is the flip-side of the classical construction of vision in which the viewing subject stands at the node of a homolographic, mathematically coherent universe. (pp. 73–74)

The switching to and fro of Žižek's anamorphic reading, like Collins' "flip-side," is not exclusionary. Rather than refute centric viewing, its distortion of one image as the other is corrected represents a reflexive research process that exposes a blurred, liminal, in-between space, a dialectical gap—an interstitial wound of visual abstraction where critical intervention and the deconstruction of the spectacle gaze can occur and where decentered, eccentric perspectives and interpretations are possible.

A dis-eased anamorphic pedagogy may also consist of a *protracted stain*, a comprehensive wounding of spectacle in the form of visual abstraction, which pervades the entire planar surface of a picture as seen in Vincent Van Gogh's *The Starry Night* (1889), Edvard Munch's *The Scream* (1893), Pablo Picasso's *Les Demoiselles d'Avignon* (1907), Jackson Pollock's *Blue Poles: Number 11* (1952), and other examples of protracted stain are found in the disjunctive narrative spaces in artwork ranging from Pablo Picasso's collage *Still Life with Piano* (1911) to Paul Citroen's photomontage *Metropolis* (1923) to Robert Rauschenberg's "combine" *Talisman* (1958) to Marina Abramović's live performance *Balkan Baroque* (1997) to Naum June Paik's and Bill Viola's counterspectacle video installations. Through their spatial and temporal strategies of abstraction, these artists compel a to and fro, anamorphic reading between their artwork and the representational assumptions of the larger historical and cultural contexts of spectacle culture. Unlike Holbein's stain, which is aberrant within the context of a single work, the protracted stains that constitute the entirety of the aforementioned artists' works are aberrant within the global economy of the mass media.

The trope "protracted stain" comes from Žižek (1997), who argues that its "uncanny 'massiveness' [in the work of modern and contemporary artists] pertains neither to the direct materiality of the...[formal properties in their works] nor to the materiality of the depicted objects—it dwells in a kind of intermediate spectral domain" (p. 32). That domain, an in-between space like Seltzer's (1997) concept of the wound, exposes and enables a critical examination of a "traumatic *yielding* to representation...that poses a radical breakdown as to the determination of the subject" (pp. 12, 11).

Of Serbian and Montenegrin decent, Abramović performed *Balkan Baroque* at the Forty-Seventh Venice Biennale, *Future Past Present*, in 1997 to grieve and heal the wounds of the devastating war in the Balkans. Her dis-eased, eccentric switching to and fro between a large pile of bones whose bits and pieces of raw flesh, which she scrubs with a coarse brush, and the other disparate images, ideas, and actions in her performance, are examples of how her disjunctive collage narrative, combined with the anamorphic reading within their in-between spaces, offers possibilities for deflecting and deconstructing the gaze of spectacle culture:

> Abramovic's approach is both tragic and wildly ironic. When she originally accepted the invitation to represent Yugoslavia, Abramovic thought hard about her homeland's responsibility for the war. She was also aware that she was the first woman to represent her homeland in Venice [at the Biennale where she performed *Balkan Baroque*], so she kept in mind that women, both Muslim and Christian, were the major victims of the violence in the war. (Watanbe, n.d., Electric version)

Video artist Bill Viola's 34-minute high-definition (HDTV) video installation *Going Forth By Day: "The Deluge"* (2002) serves as a counterspectacle to disaster tourism. Compared with the constant stream of mass mediated images of the tsunami and Hurricane Katrina that flooded peoples' homes worldwide, Viola's surround movie is ironic and uncanny. It begins with a still image of a façade.

Then, movement appears as people walk along the street, then run along the street rapidly passing by, then people pour down the front stairway and out the door in a state of panic, then their rush is forced by a tremendous wave of water that thrusts down the stairway carrying submerged bodies with it out the front door, and onto the street.

And finally, the remainder of the 65,000 gallons of water in Viola's set continues to flow out of the door and the windows of the house. The montage of ambient sounds and moving images in *The Deluge* surround viewers within the four, 7-foot high projection walls of the installation, which Viola describes as a "walk-in movie":

> It's the [to and fro] movement of the viewer in the space that unfolds the narrative, which is what goes on in fresco cycles. People are free to linger where they want. When you liberate the image from fixed seats and the proscenium arch, you engage the viewer's body, and the relationship to the image becomes much more personal. (Wolff, 2002, Electronic version)

Figure 8.1. Bill Viola, *Going Forth By Day:* "*The Deluge,*" 2002a. Video still courtesy James Cohan Gallery, New York.

Figure 8.2. Bill Viola, *Going Forth By Day:* "*The Deluge,*" 2002b. Video still courtesy James Cohan Gallery, New York.

Figure 8.3. Bill Viola, *Going Forth By Day*: "*The Deluge*," 2002c. Video still courtesy James Cohan Gallery, New York.

While the awesome force *of* and *in* the moving images is stunning, Viola's visual and aural inversion of a deluge thrusting *out of a house rather than into it* engages viewers' bodies in a protracted time and space, which when read anamorphically deconstructs the gaze of disaster tourism and enables subjective interpretations based on the dis-eased flow of their personal memories and cultural histories.

Whether an aberrant stain within the context of a specific artwork such as *The Ambassadors* or a protracted stain within the global context of visual culture such as *Balkan Baroque* and *The Deluge*, the pedagogical distortion of anamorphosis "complements what geometral researches into perspective allow to escape from vision," according to psychoanalytic theorist Jacque Lacan (1981, p. 87). Building on Lacanian theory, linguistic theorist Patrick Fuery (1995) argues that the "invisibility of representation, which is also [the] absence of subjectivity and this loss, is why the image/sign [spectacle] operates as a trap [for the gaze]" (p. 134). In other words, the gaze of spectacle culture finds its power in creating a lack, an open wound wherein it can infect and colonize viewers' subjectivities. Fuery characterizes this lack as "allurement...":

> ...[namely] the creation of an operational absence as a desire in the gaze. It is the transformation of the sign so that it becomes irresistible to the gaze, not simply as a point of attraction, but as a focal point. The lure is an exaggeration, an excess which threatens to topple over into its own sense of sign-ness, and in doing so to lose is capacity to capture and become the tain [the back of a mirror] of specula(tive)r action. The lure must draw attention to itself, and at the same time disguise this very action—this quality is lost once the eye becomes aware of the allurement. (p. 132)

Like the stretch of St. Bartholomew's flayed skin in Michelangelo's ironic self-portrait in *The Last Judgment* (1535–1541) or the wounded landscapes of photographer Richard Misrach, anamorphism is an open visual and conceptual wound that resists the allure of spectacle. Its eccentric visuality ruptures our perceptual and cognitive understandings. Considering this ability to disrupt normalized assumptions, it has the potential to foster a critical engagement with spectacle culture. As critical pedagogy, the eccentricity of anamorphic reading challenges the lure of and obsession (trap) with the commodity fetishism of spectacle culture thus enabling its deconstruction through viewers' intervention and performances of subjectivity. Against the lure and trap of its wound culture, the to and fro of anamorphic reading constitutes a *suturing/de-suturing* process—a performance of subjectivity that continually deconstructs and reconstructs the hegemony of spectacle through misrecognition (*méconnaisance*).

Suturing, according to Lacan (1981), is the "conjunction of the imaginary and the symbolic," the tie of the spectator's subjectivity with the narrative of spectacle (p. 118). De-suturing is the process where the seam that ties the spectator with the narrative is "ripped open," thus exposing "the fabrication of the illusion of whole-ness of both the spectator and the [spectacle]" (Herzogenrath, 1999, Electronic version). For Deleuze and Guattari (1987), de-suturing exposes "the body to connections that presuppose an entire assemblage, circuits, conjunctions, levels and thresholds, passages and distributions of intensity, and territories and deterritorializations," which make possible the deconstruction of parasitic and viral accumulations (p. 161). Hence, the eccentricity of suturing/de-suturing enables the examination and critique of visually coherent systems and constitutes subjectivity as open and mutable.

In the film *A Clockwork Orange* (1971) by Stanley Kubrick, the antagonist Alex's obsession with violence suggests his loss of subjectivity due to an imbalance in the suturing/de-suturing of the Lacanian Imaginary and the Symbolic. Lacking such eccentric visuality, Alex has fallen into the realm of the Lacanian Real, into psychosis, where his disaster tourism has crossed over to perpetrating actual violence. To purge his terrorist impulses, clinicians tie him to a chair and force him to watch horrifying films by means of the "Ludovico Technique," the film's fictitious therapy intended to inflict an abhorrent, sick feeling at the sight of any violence. With his eyes "clamped open and constantly eye-dropped," Alex is subjected to this Pavlovian form of psychological conditioning to prevent even "the slightest aversion [any eccentric to and fro] to the terrible images on the screen." An anamorphic reading of *A Clockwork Orange* suggests Kubrick

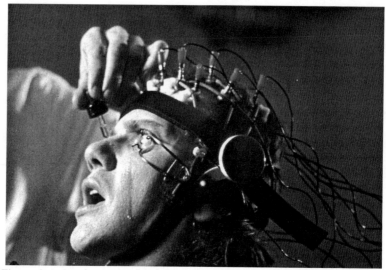

Figure 8.4. Stanley Kubrick, *A Clockwork Orange*, 1971. Film still courtesy Photofest.

created this scene as an "aberrant stain" to call into question the pathological violence depicted throughout the film in particular, as well as that of the pathological public sphere of spectacle culture in general, where an imbalance between the Imaginary and the Symbolic can lead to psychosis.

Ironically, while the aim of the Ludovico Technique in *A Clockwork Orange* was to transform the dis-eased and volatile Alex into a docile body (Foucault, 1995, p. 136), that of the critical pedagogy of anamorphism is eccentric subjectivity, a contrary, dis-eased positioning of the body that challenges the politicizing gaze of disaster tourism and makes critical multiperspectival readings and interpretations of media spectacle possible. Contrary to therapies that expose (wound), objectify, classify, and conform (suture) the body to the politics and the commodity marketplace of mass spectacle, the eccentric de-suturing/re-suturing pedagogy of critical anamorphism is an ontological process whereby the gaze of spectacle culture is deconstructed and reconstructed thus enabling creative and political agency through a multiplicity of experiences, perspectives, and understandings that constitute the subjectivity of critical citizenship.

Notes

One. The Embodied Pedagogy of War

1. With the unconventional typographic design of this chapter we pay homage to the eccentric collage inventions of the Dadaists who used various fonts, unorthodox punctuation, inconsistent spacing, and unusual printing symbols to experiment with print culture and to critique and wage war against the technological violence of World War I. The resultant visual, textual, and conceptual vertigo experienced from these disjunctions constitutes a performative strategy that we use in this chapter to critique the spectacle of visual culture, which is implicated in the war with Iraq.

Two. The Spectacle of Visual Culture

1. A contemporary example of "romanticized resistances" is found in the aestheticization of dissent by the Democratic Party, which in its treatment of a public figure such as Howard Dean has vilified his radical political critique as threatening, disruptive, and hence unacceptable.

2. In this section, the arguments regarding spectacle pedagogy shift from those supported by the writings of critical theorists to the "theories" posited by artists and movements in the historical and contemporary *avant-garde* that have critiqued the spectacle of visual culture through creative work. Our aim is to present artwork as theoretical explorations rather than merely illustrations of theory. The final section of this essay returns to a more conventional presentation of theoretical arguments.

Five. Misfit Pedagogy of Visual Culture: A Depraved Obsession with Pictures

1. Bentham conceived of the Panopticon in 1791 as a prison design that would enable the guards to keep inmates under constant surveillance by

gazing into their cells from a central tower. Because the guards would be concealed in the central tower, the inmates would not know they were being watched.

Seven. The Spectre of Visual Culture and the Hauntology of Collage

1. See also Gilles Deleuze and Félix Guattari's (1987, p. 98) conceptualization of language as "stammering." Radical educator Kaustuv Roy (2003, pp. 122–123) argues that Deleuze's concept of creative stammering opens pedagogical spaces wherein its linguistic disorientations and dissidences enable an examination and experimentation of signs.

2. Howard Gardner (1985, p. 95) also writes about the disjunctive narrative of television and the disruption of commercial advertising.

3. The role of the public intellectual is "to present alternative narratives and other perspectives on history than those provided by the combatants on behalf of official memory and national identity—who tend to work in terms of falsified unities, the manipulation of demonized or distorted representations of undesirable and/or excluded populations," claims Said (2001, p. 6).

Eight. The Dis-eased Pedagogy of Disaster Tourism

1. As told to Thierry Bardini at the *Conférence Terreurs, Terrorismes et Mécanismes Inconscients*, Montréal, October 31, 2005). See Bardini (2006, no. 3).

2. According to *The Oxford English Dictionary* (Electronic version) the prefix *dis* is defined as "removal, aversion, negation," and *dis-ease* means "absence of ease; uneasiness, discomfort; inconvenience, annoyance; disquiet, disturbance; trouble." Hence "dis-ease" as we used it here is double coded. On the one hand, we are referring to the *disabling* of the body's agency and health due to its marginalization as other within contemporary cultural life. On the other hand, we are referring to the *enabling* of the body's agency through its eccentric and reflexive examination and critique of centric, oppressive cultural assumptions.

3. Hayles (1999) defines "*informatics* [as] the technologies of information as well as the biological, social, linguistic, and cultural changes that initiate, accompany, and complicate their development" (p. 29).

4. This is our emphasis to underscore the sublime ideological project of spectacle culture.

References

Adorno, T. (1991). *The culture industry*. London: Routledge.

Associated Press. (2005, December 15). Tourist attraction focuses on Katrina destruction. Retrieved January 5, 2006, from: http://www.cnn.com/2005/US/12/15/katrina.tour.ap.ap/?eref =yahoo

Bakhtin. M. (1984). *Rabelais and his world*. H. Iswolsky (Trans.). Bloomington: Indiana University Press.

Bardini, T. (2006, February 2). Hypervirus: A clinical report. *C-Theory*. Retrieved February 14, 2006, from: http://www. ctheory.net/articles.aspx?id=504

Barrow, J. D. (1998). *Impossibility: The limits of science and the science of limits*. London: Oxford University Press.

Barthelme, D. (1997). *Not-knowing: The essays and interviews of Donald Barthelme*. K. Harzinger (Ed.). New York: Random House.

Barthes, R. (1974) S/Z. R. Miller (Trans.) New York: Hill & Wang.

Barthes, R. (1977). *Mythologies*. New York: Hill & Wang.

Barthes, R. (1991). *Camera lucida: Reflections on photography*. New York: Hill & Wang.

Bateson, G. (1972). *Steps to an ecology of mind*. New York: Ballantine.

Baudrillard, J. (1994). *Simulacra and simulation*. Ann Arbor: University of Michigan Press.

Baudrillard, J. (2002a). *The spirit of terrorism and requiem for the Twin Towers*. C. Turner (Trans.). London: Verso.

Baudrillard, J. (2002b). *The transparency of evil: Essays on extreme phenomena.* J. Benedict (Trans.). London: Verso.

Beaudoin, T. (2005, April 2). Op-Ed: Tragic Schiavo case epitomized American cult of celebrity. *Centre Daily Times,* p. A10.

Becker, C. (2002). *Surpassing the spectacle: Global transformations and the changing politics of art.* Lanham: Rowan and Littlefield.

Benjamin, W. (1968). The storyteller. In H. Arendt (Ed.), *Illuminations: Walter Benjamin, essays and reflections* (pp. 83–109). New York: Schocken.

Benjamin, W. (1999). *The Arcades Project.* H. Eiland & K. McLaughlin (Trans). Cambridge: Belknap Press.

Bernhard, B. (1998, June 24). Calamity of excellence: Lawrence Weschler laments the loss of journalism that asks for nothing but our attention. *LA Weekly.* [Electronic version]. Retrieved March 17, 2004, from: http://www.laweekly.com/ink/printme.php?eid=1565

Bhabha, H. K. (1994). *The location of culture.* London: Routledge.

Boorstin, D. J. (1987). *The image: A guide to pseudo-events in America.* New York: Atheneum.

Bottoms, S. J. (2000, October). *Biochemically stressed: Goat Island, the body, technology and poison.* Paper presented at the Performative Sites: Intersecting Art, Technology, and the Body Symposium at The Pennsylvania State University, University Park, Pennsylvania.

Boulding, K. E. (1961). *The image: Knowledge in life and society.* Ann Arbor: University of Michigan Press.

Bourdieu, P. (1990). *The logic of practice.* Stanford, CA: Stanford University Press.

Bowers, C. A. (1993). *Critical essays on education, modernity, and the recovery of the ecological imperative.* New York: Teachers College Press.

Brockelman, T. (2001). *The frame and the mirror: On collage and the postmodern.* Evanston: Northwestern University Press.

Brown, N. C. M. (2003). Are we entering a post-critical age in visual arts education? *Studies in Art Education, 44*(3), 285–289.

Burke, E. (1998). *A philosophical inquiry.* Oxford: Oxford University Press.

Carse, J. P. (1986). *Finite and infinite games.* New York: Free Press.

CBS News. (2004, June 10). Report: Rumsfeld OK'd prison rules. Retrieved July 15, 2004 from: http://www. cbsnews. com/ stories/ 2004/06/11/iraq/ main622522.shtml

Chapman, L. H. (2003). Studies of the mass arts. *Studies in Art Education, 44*(3), 230–245.

Cimbala, S. J. (2004, May 17). Abu Graib reveals U.S. culture. *Centre Daily Times,* p. A6.

Clandinin, D. J. & Connelly, F. M. (2000). *Narrative inquiry: Experience and story in qualitative research.* San Francisco: Jossey-Bass.

CNN.com. (2005, January 31). Retrieved February 21, 2005, from: http://www.cnn.com/2005/EDUCATION/01/31/students.amendment.ap/

Coleridge, S. T. (1817/1985). Biographia literaria. In J. Engell & W. J. Bate (Eds.), *The collected works of Samuel Taylor Coleridge, Vol. 7.* Princeton, NJ: Princeton University Press.

Collins, D. (1992). Anamorphosis and the eccentric observer: Inverted perspective and construction of the gaze. *Leonardo, 25*(1), 73–82.

De Moraes, L. (2005, November 3). Anderson Cooper, CNN's man of the hour. *Washington Post.* Retrived November 19, 2005, from: http://www.washingtonpost.com/wp-dyn/ content/article/2005/11/02/AR2005110203079.html

Debord, G. (1994). *The society of the spectacle.* D. Nicholson-Smith (Trans.). New York: Zone.

Deleuze, G. (1994). He stuttered. In C. V. Boundas & D. Olkowski (Eds.), *Gilles Deleuze and the Theater of Philosophy* (pp. 23–29). New York: Routledge.

Deleuze, G. (1995). *Negotiations*. M. Joughin (Trans.). New York: Columbia University Press.

Deleuze, G. & Guattari, F. (1983). *Anti-Oedipus: Capitalism and schizophrenia*. Minneapolis: University of Minnesota Press.

Deleuze, G., & Guattari, F. (1987). *A thousand plateaus: Capitalism and schizophrenia*. B. Massumi (Trans.). Minneapolis: University of Minnesota Press.

Dennis, D. (2001, Sept. 18). The world trade center and the rise of the security state. *CTHEORY: Theory, technology and culture, 24*(3). [Electronic version]. Retrieved Oct. 3, 2001, from: http://www.ctheory.net/

Derrida, J. (1994). *Specters of Marx: The state of the debt, the work of mourning, and the new international*. P. Kamuf (Trans.). New York: Routledge.

Ehrenreich, B. (2004). Barnard College 2004 commencement: Author Barbara Ehrenreich calls for new kind of feminism to counter images of prison abuse. Retrieved May 29, 2004, from: http://www.ascribe.org/cgibin/spew4th.pl?ascribeid=20040521.122630&time=12%2042%20PDT&year=2004&public=1

Ellsworth, E. (1997). *Teaching positions: Difference, pedagogy, and the power of address*. New York: Teachers College Press.

Esmail-Hudani, S. (2004, May 17). *Inside Abu Ghraib: The violence of the camera*. Retrieved May 29, 2004, from: http://www.counterpunch.org/hudani05172004.html

Feasey, R. D. (n.d.). *Last action hero*. Retrieved March 24, 2004, from: http://www.nottingham.ac.uk/film/journal/filmrev/last-action-hero.htm

Felman, S. (1987). *Jacques Lacan and the adventure of insight: Psychoanalysis in contemporary culture*. Cambridge, MA: Harvard University Press.

Felman, S. (1992). Education and crisis, or the vicissitudes of teaching. In S. Felman & D. Laub (Eds.), *Testimony: Crises of witnessing in literature, psychoanalysis, and history* (pp. 1–56). New York: Routledge.

Fiske, J. (1992). Cultural studies and the culture of everyday life. In L. Grossberg, C. Nelson, & P. Treichler (Eds.), *Cultural studies* (pp. 154–173). New York: Routledge.

Forkscrew, (n.d.). Retrieved July 15, 2004, from: http://www.Forkscrew.com

Foucault, M. (1972). *The archaeology of knowledge: And the discourse on language.* New York: Pantheon.

Foucault, M. (1994). *The birth of the clinic: An archaeology of medical perception.* New York: Vintage.

Foucault, M. (1995). *Discipline and punish: The birth of the prison.* A. Sheridan (Trans.). New York: Vintage.

Freedberg, D. (1989). *The power of images: Studies in the history and theory of response.* Chicago: University of Chicago Press.

Freedman, K. (2003). *Teaching visual culture: Curriculum, aesthetics, and the social life of art.* New York: Teachers College Press.

Fuery, P. (1995). *The theory of absence: Subjectivity, signification, and desire.* Westport, CT: Greenwood.

Gablik, S. (1991). *The reenchantment of art.* London: Thames & Hudson.

Gadamer, H.-G. (1986). *The relevance of the beautiful and other essays.* Cambridge, England: Cambridge University Press.

Gadamer, H.-G. (1989). *Truth and method.* London: Sheed & Ward.

Gardner, H. (1985). Cracking the codes of television: The child as anthropologist. In P. D'Agostino (Ed.), *Transmission: Theory and practice for a new television aesthetics* (pp. 93–102). New York: Tanam.

Garoian, C. (1999). *Performing pedagogy: Toward an art of politics*. Albany: State University of New York Press.

Garoian, C. (2002, Fall). Performing a pedagogy of endurance. *Teacher Education Quarterly*, 29(4), 161–173.

Giroux, H. (1996). *Fugitive cultures: Race, violence, and youth*. New York: Routledge.

Giroux, H. A. (1997). *Pedagogy and the politics of hope: Theory, culture, and schooling*. Boulder, CO: Westview.

Giroux, H. A. & Simon, R. I. (1989). Schooling, popular culture, and pedagogy of possibility. In H. A. Giroux & R. I. Simon (Eds), *Popular culture: Schooling and everyday life* (pp. 219–236. New York: Bergin & Garvey.

Goat Island. (1998). *The impossible & poison and 37 squared: A reading companion to the sea & poison*. Chicago: Goat Island.

Harper, R. (2002, Sept.). We can rebuild you. *Wired*, pp. 54–55.

Hayles, N. K. (1999). *How we became posthuman: Virtual bodies in cybernetics, literature, and informatics*. Chicago: University of Chicago Press.

Herman, E. S. & Chomsky, N. (1988). *Manufacturing consent: The political economy of the mass media*. New York: Pantheon.

Hersh, S. M. (2004a, May 10). Torture at Abu Ghraib: American soldiers brutalized Iraqis. How far up does the responsibility go? *New Yorker*, pp. 42–47.

Hersh, S. M. (2004b, May 17). Chain of command: How the Department of Defense mishandled the disaster at Abu Ghraib. *New Yorker*, pp. 38–43.

Hersh, S. M. (2004c, May 24). The gray zone: The secret Pentagon program at Abu Ghraib. *New Yorker*, pp. 38–44.

Herzogenrath, B. (1999, Jan.). On the *Lost Highway*: Lynch and Lacan, cinema and cultural pathology. *Other Voices: The (e)Journal of Cultural Criticism, 1*(3). [Electronic version]. Retrieved January 5, 2006, from: http://www.othervoices. org/1.3/bh/highway.html

hooks, b. (1996). *Reel to real: Race, sex, and class at the movies.* New York: Routledge.

Hucheon, L. (1985). *The theory of parody: The teachings of twentieth-century art forms.* New York: Methuen.

Illich, I. (1976). *Medical nemesis: The expropriation of health.* New York: Pantheon.

jagodzinski, j. (2003). Unromancing the stone of "resistance": In defence of a continued radical politics in visual cultural studies. *Journal of Social Theory in Art Education,* (23), 104–139.

Jay, M. (1988). Scopic regimes of modernity. In H. Foster (Ed.), *Vision and visuality* (pp. 3–23). Seattle, WA: Bay Press.

Juergensmeyer, M. (2000). *Terror in the mind of God: The global rise of religious violence.* Berkeley: University of California Press.

Kahn, J. (2003, March). Stripped for parts. *Wired,* pp. 132–137.

Kindler, A. M. (2003). Visual culture, visual brain and (art) education. *Studies in Art Education, 44*(3), 290–295.

Kirshenblatt-Gimblett, B. (1998). Destination culture: Tourism, museums, and heritage. Berkeley: University of California Press.

Kracauer, S. (1963/1995). *The mass ornament: Weimar essays.* Cambridge, MA: Harvard University Press.

Kroker, A. & Kroker, M. (2001, Sept. 18). Terrorism of viral power. *CTHEORY: Theory, technology and culture, 24*(3). [Electronic version]. Retrieved October 3, 2001, from: http://www.ctheory.net/

Kuenzli, R. (2005) Exhibition panels: *Interventionist collage: From Dada to the present.* Iowa City: University of Iowa Museum of Art.

Kuspit, D. (1983). Collage: The organizing principle of art in the age of the relativity of art. In B. J. Craige (Ed.), *Relativism in the arts* (pp. 123–147). Athens: University of Georgia Press.

Lacan, J. (1977). *Écrits: A selection.* A. Sheridan (Trans.). New York: Norton.

Lacan, J. (1981). *The four fundamental concepts of psychoanalysis.* New York: Norton.

Lasch, C. (1991). *The culture of narcissism: American life in an age of diminishing expectations.* New York: Norton.

Lazzarato, M. (1996). Immaterial labor. In P. Virno & M. Hardt (Eds.), *Radical thought in Italy: A potential politics* (pp. 132–146). Minneapolis: University of Minnesota Press.

Lennon, J., & Foley, M. (2000). *Dark tourism: The attraction of death and disaster.* London: Continuum.

Leopold, A. (1970). *A sand county almanac.* San Francisco: Ballantine.

Levy, S. (n.d.). Stacy Levy. Retrieved from: http://www.stacylevy.com/installations/testing_the_waters.php

Lorde, A. (1984). The transformation of silence into language and action. In A. Lorde, *Sister Outsider: Essays and Speeches* (pp. 40–44). Trumansburg, NY: Crossing Press.

Mailer, N. (2005, January 23). One idea. *Parade.* New York: Parade.

Marcuse, H. (1972). *One dimensional man.* London: Abacus.

May, R. (1975). *The courage to create.* New York: Norton.

McKenzie, J. (2001). *Perform or else: From to discipline to performance.* London: Routledge.

McLuhan, M. (1964). *Understanding media: The extensions of man.* New York: Signet.

McQuillan, M. (2000). Introduction. In M. McQuillan (Ed.), *The narrative reader* (pp. 1–33). London: Routledge.

Menand, L. (2004, January 5). Masters of the matrix: Kennedy, Nixon, and the culture of the image. *New Yorker*, pp. 82–86.

Meyer, D. (2004, May 16). Rush: MPs just "blowing off steam." CBS News.com: *Against the grain*. Retrieved July 15, 2004, from: http://www.cbsnews.com/stories/2004/05/06/opinion/meyer/main616021.shtml

Miller, N. (n.d.). Hauntology and history in Jacques Derrida's *Spectres of Marx*. Retrieved July 17, 2004, from: http://www.nodo50.org/cubasigloXXI/taller/miller_100304.pdf

Minh-ha, T. T. (1999). *Cinema interval*. New York: Routledge.

Mirzoeff, N. (1995). *Bodyscape: Art, modernity, and the ideal figure*. London: Routledge.

Mitchell, T. (1998). Orientalism and the exhibitionary order. In N. Mirzoeff (Ed.), *The Visual Culture Reader* (pp. 293–303). London: Routledge.

Mitchell, W. J. T. (1994). *Picture theory*. Chicago: University of Chicago Press.

Nietzsche, F. (1957). *The use and abuse of history*. A. Collins (Trans.). Indianapolis: Bobbs-Merrill.

Oxford English Dictionary. Retrieved February 13, 2003, from: http://dictionary.oed.com.ezaccess.libraries.psu.edu/cgi/entry/50064802?query_type=word&queryword=dis&first=1&max_to_show=10&sort_type=alpha&search_id=BABv-0PLxKk-1420&result_place=2

Palmer, P. J. (1998). *The courage to teach: Exploring the inner landscape of a teacher's life*. San Francisco, CA: Jossey-Bass.

Phillips, P. C. (2003). Creating democracy: A dialogue with Krzysztof Wodiczko. *Art Journal, 63*(4), 32-49.

Polanyi, M. (1983). *The tacit dimension*. Gloucester, MA: Smith.

Prakash, M. S. (1993). Gandhi's postmodern education: Ecology, peace, and multiculturalism relinked. *Holistic Education Review, 6* (3), 8–17.

Radical Left.net. (2005). Retrieved November 19, 2005, from: http://www.radicalleft.net/blog/_archives/2005/3/30/485846. html

Rapoport, A. (1967). Escape from paradox. *Scientific American, 217* (1), 50–56.

Rorty, R. (1979). *Philosophy and the mirror of nature.* Princeton, NJ: Princeton University Press.

Ross, A. (1994). The ecology of images. In N. Bryson, M. Holly, & K. Moxley (Eds.), *Visual culture: Images and interpretations* (pp. 325–346). Hanover, NH: University Press of New England.

Roy, K. (2003). *Teachers in nomadic spaces: Deleuze and curriculum.* New York: Lang.

Said, E. W. (2001, September 11). The public role of writers and intellectuals. *The Nation.* Retrieved January 12, 2005, from: http://www.thenation.com/doc/20010917/essay

Schneider, R. (1997). *The explicit body in performance.* New York: Routledge.

Seltzer, M. (1997, Spring). Wound culture: Trauma in the pathological public sphere. *October, 80,* 3–36.

Semetsky, I. (2003). An unconscious subject of Deleuze and Guattari. Retrieved January 13, 2005, from: http:// www. arts.monash.edu/cclcs/research/papers/pdf/Unconscious_ Subject.pdf

Sontag, S. (1966). *Against interpretation.* New York: Farrar, Straus & Giroux.

Sontag, S. (1969). *Styles of radical will.* New York: Dell.

Sontag, S. (1977). *On photography.* New York: Farrar, Straus & Giroux.

Sontag, S. (1978). *Illness as metaphor.* New York: Farrar, Straus & Giroux.

Sontag, S. (1980). *Under the sign of Saturn.* New York: Farrar, Straus & Giroux.

Sontag, S. (2004, May 23). Regarding the torture of others: Notes on what has been done—and why—to prisoners, by Americans. *New York Times Magazine*, sec. 6, pp. 24–29, 42.

Sullivan, A. (2003, Oct. 20). Pumping irony. *Time, 162*(16), p. 88.

Takemoto, T. (2003). The melancholia of AIDS: Interview with Douglas Crimp. *Art Journal, 62*(4), 80–91.

Tavin, K. (2003). Wrestling with angels, searching for ghosts: Toward a critical pedagogy of visual culture. *Studies in Art Education, 44*(3), 197–213.

Ulmer, G. L. (1983). The object of post-criticism. In H. Foster (Ed.), *The anti-aesthetic: Essays on postmodern culture* (pp. 83–110). Seattle: Bay Press.

United Nations, Office of the High Commissioner for Human Rights. (1949). Geneva Convention relative to the treatment of prisoners of war. Retrieved July 15, 2004, from: http://www.unhchr.ch/html/menu3/b/91.html

Virilio, P. (2000). *Art and fear.* London: Continuum.

Watanabe, S. (n.d.). The influence of the nation-state on art: The case of the former Yugoslavian countries. Retrieved April 19, 2006, from: http://www.spikyart.org/nationstate/ nation-stateintroduction.htm and http://www.spikyart.org/ nation-state/thesis5.html

Wilson, B. (2003). Of diagrams and rhizomes: Visual culture, contemporary art, and the impossibility of mapping the content of art education. *Studies in Art Education, 44*(3), 214–229.

Wodiczko, K. (n.d.). Krzysztof Wodiczko. Retrieved March 25, 2004, from: http://www.mit.edu:8001/afs/athena.mit.edu/ course/4/4.395/www/krystof/krystof.html

Wolff, E. (2002, February 1). Digital cathedral: An artist ahead of his time. Retrieved January 5, 2006, from: http://millimeter.com/mag/video_digital_cathedral/index.html

Young, D. (2005). *Frequency and flow*. Correspondence with artist and teacher David Young regarding his assemblage.

Žižek, S. (1989). *The sublime object of ideology*. London: Verso.
Žižek, S. (1997). *The plague of fantasies*. London: Verso.

Žižek, S. (2004, May 21). What Rumsfeld doesn't know that he knows about Abu Ghraib. Retrieved July 20, 2004, from: http://www.inthesetimes.com/article/747

Index

Note: Page numbers with an *f* indicate figures.

Index

Index   163

advertising on, 102
Baudrillard on, 32
disaster coverage on, 119–121
Gardner on, 142n2
Mailer on, 102
reality, 31, 75, 81
war-making and, 77–78
terrorism, 3, 34, 109
artistic, 59
corporate, 84
ecological, 42–44, 54, 59–61
Geneva Conventions and, 80
pedagogical, 108, 126
performative acts of, 79
spectacle of, 125–127
"virus" of, 44
See also September 11th attacks
testing, standardized, 101–102
theatricality, 75. See also spectacle
"Third Space of enunciation," 67, 92, 93, 97
Tiller Girls, 25
Titan Corporation, 77
torture, 74–77, 109
tourism, disaster, 6, 119–126, 134, 139–140
transcontextuality, 52
transgression, 33
pedagogic, 27–28, 32
transformation and, 27–28, 37–39, 124–125

transplants, organ, 21
tsunami, 109, 119–120, 134
tuberculosis, 129
TV Buddha (Paik), 94–97, 95f

Ulmer, Gregory, 3, 89, 93

Van Gogh, Vincent, 133
Venice Biennale, 133–134
Vesalius, Andreas, 128
video art, 63, 64
Vietnam War, 33
Vintondale, PA, 104–107, 105f, 106f
Viola, Bill, 133–138, 135f–137f
virality, 43, 44, 124, 126–127
Virilio, Paul, 101, 117
voyeurism, 23, 32, 68, 121. See also gaze

Watanbe, S., 134
Weschler, Lawrence, 26
Wilson, Elizabeth, 27–28
Wired magazine, 7, 9–21
Wodiczko, Krzysztof, 33–36, 35f
Wojnarowicz, David, 33
World Trade Center. See September 11th attacks

Young, David, 111–114, 112f, 113f

Žižek, Slavoj, 75–76, 131–133